A CAPELL FAMILY BOOK

THE SCOTT AND LAURIE OKI SERIES IN ASIAN AMERICAN STUDIES

A Principled Stand

THE STORY OF *HIRABAYASHI V. UNITED STATES*

GORDON K. HIRABAYASHI

with James A. Hirabayashi
and Lane Ryo Hirabayashi

A Capell Family Book

The Scott and Laurie Oki Series in Asian American Studies

UNIVERSITY OF WASHINGTON PRESS
Seattle & London

Publication of A Principled Stand *is made possible in part by grants from the Scott and Laurie Oki Endowed Fund, which publishes books in Asian American studies, and the Capell Family Endowed Book Fund, which supports the publication of books that deepen the understanding of social justice through historical, cultural, and environmental studies.*

The book also received generous support from the George and Sakaye Aratani Professorship in Japanese American Redress, Incarceration, and Community, at UCLA.

A full listing of the books in the Oki Series can be found at the back of the book.

Printed and bound in the United States of America
Design by Thomas Eykemans
Composed in Chaparral, typeface designed by Carol Twolmby
16 15 14 13   5 4 3 2 1

UNIVERSITY OF WASHINGTON PRESS
PO Box 50096, Seattle, WA 98145, USA
www.washington.edu/uwpress

LIBRARY OF CONGRESS CATALOGING-IN-PUBLICATION DATA
Hirabayashi, Gordon K.
A principled stand : the story of Hirabayashi v. United States / Gordon K. Hirabayashi with James A. Hirabayashi and Lane Ryo Hirabayashi.
      p. cm. (Scott and Laurie Oki series in Asian American studies and Capell family book)
Includes bibliographical references and index.
ISBN 978-0-295-99270-9 (cloth : alk. paper)
1. Hirabayashi, Gordon K.—Trials, litigation, etc. 2. Japanese Americans—Evacuation and relocation, 1942–1945. 3. Japanese Americans—Legal status, laws, etc. 4. Japanese Americans—Civil rights. 5. United States. Constitution. 5th Amendment. I. Hirabayashi, James A. II. Hirabayashi, Lane Ryo. III. Title.
KF228.H565H57 2013   341.6'7—dc23   2012038855

The paper used in this publication is acid-free and meets the minimum requirements of American National Standard for Information Sciences—Permanence of Paper for Printed Library Materials, ANSI Z39.48–1984.∞

341.6
H

This book is dedicated in loving memory to my

Uncle Gordon Kiyoshi Hirabayashi (1918–2012)

Aunt Esther Hirabayashi [Nee Schmoe] (1924–2012)

Father, James Akira Hirabayashi (1926–2012)

Lane Ryo Hirabayashi

CONTENTS

Preface   *ix*

Acknowledgments   *xvii*

Acronyms   *xix*

PART I. AN ISSEI-NISEI FAMILY   *3*

1. Hotaka to Seattle   *11*
2. Growing Up in America   *25*
3. "You're Going to College"   *43*

PART II. CHALLENGES AND INCARCERATION   *53*

4. World War II   *55*
5. Arraignment Summons   *66*
6. King County Jail   *73*
7. King County Jail Mates   *84*
8. Jail Visitations   *92*
9. World War II Interracial Marriage   *99*
10. Prison Meditations   *103*
11. Pretrial   *117*
12. Seattle Federal District Court   *123*
13. U.S. Supreme Court   *132*
14. Out on Bail   *137*
15. Thumbing to Jail   *145*
16. Catalina Federal Honor Camp   *150*
17. Federal Prison Again   *160*

PART III. THE POSTWAR YEARS AND VINDICATION   167

18. Early Postwar Experiences   173
19. *Coram Nobis*   181

Appendix 1. Major Publications   191
Appendix 2. Professional Positions, Honors, and Awards   193
Glossary of Names   197
Further Reading   201
About the Coauthors   205
Index   207

PREFACE

GORDON KIYOSHI HIRABAYASHI (1918–2012) IS BEST KNOWN for being one of three Japanese Americans whose legal challenges to the curfew imposed on and the subsequent removal of Japanese Americans from their homes reached the U.S. Supreme Court during the 1940s. We wrote *A Principled Stand* in order to complement the many publications that examine Gordon's court cases. While most of the available literature focuses on the legal aspects of his resistance, our focus is on Gordon as a person. We use his own words to try to convey what inspired him to challenge the federal government during World War II.

Some forty years after Gordon's initial trials, legal historian Peter Irons and a team made up mainly of young lawyers born after the war revisited Gordon's conviction by utilizing a rare doctrine—writ of error *coram nobis*—to reopen his case. Their ultimate victory enhanced Gordon's reputation as a resister. He was not only heralded in the Japanese American community but also widely recognized by mainstream institutions for his principled stand during the 1940s.

The following three topics provide the background for reading Gordon's story: the origins of this project; Gordon's legal cases; and a note on the process of constructing his narrative in *A Principled Stand*.

ORIGINS OF THE PROJECT

During the 1990s, James (Jim) Hirabayashi, Gordon's younger brother, visited Gordon in Edmonton, Alberta, Canada, and recorded several interviews. In 2008, Jim returned to Canada and collected extensive personal files that were stored in Gordon's garage. After perusing the material, he came up with the idea of using these unpublished primary documents to convey Gordon's thoughts and emotions during the 1940s. He invited his son, Lane, to join him, and for three years they read, met, corresponded, and exchanged ideas on how best to carry out this task.

The purpose of this book is to convey what was going through Gordon's mind at the time. What inspired and enabled him to withstand the psychological and emotional burden of sustained, nonviolent resistance? How did he endure the challenges of taking on the federal government and its massive legal resources? Who gave him hope, and how? The pages that follow endeavor to give readers a sense of Gordon's background and the people, networks, and community organizations that framed his upbringing and life into his early twenties.

LEGAL CASES

On February 19, 1942, President Franklin D. Roosevelt issued Executive Order 9066, delegating broad powers to the secretary of war and his military commanders for the purpose of protecting national security. Although Executive Order 9066 named no specific group, it gave military commanders the right to remove any potentially dangerous, or even suspicious, individuals from military areas as well as to confine such persons if necessary. Congress backed the executive order by passing Public Law 503, which subjected civilians who violated the order to imprisonment and fines.

In February 1942, authorities decided that it was necessary to remove Japanese Americans from areas that were seen as being too close to strategic coastal waters. Japanese Americans were ordered to leave Terminal Island, California, on March 14, 1942, and move to Los Angeles proper or inland, only to be removed again, to Wartime Civil Control Administration (WCCA) camps the following month. Likewise, Japanese Americans on Bainbridge Island, Washington, were ordered to leave their homes on March 23, 1942.

On March 28, the Western Defense Command, under General John L. DeWitt, issued a proclamation that was essentially a curfew order. It confined all enemy aliens—Germans, Italians, Japanese, and what the army called "non-aliens of Japanese ancestry"—to their homes between 8 a.m. and 6 p.m. and restricted travel beyond a five-mile radius from their residences.

In April 1942, the government began to post official proclamations on telephone poles and post office bulletin boards in California and parts of Oregon, Washington, and Arizona: "NOTICE: TO ALL PERSONS OF JAPANESE ANCESTRY, BOTH ALIEN AND NON-ALIEN." These notices ordered all persons of Japanese ancestry, whether or not they were U.S. citizens, to report to the Wartime Civil Control Administration. As a result, and by governmental fiat, Japanese Americans were forced to leave their homes and communities. Under military guard, they were first transported by buses and trains to one of sixteen temporary WCCA detention camps, euphemistically called "assembly centers," most of which were in California. Horse stables and crudely built barracks served as mass housing for tens of thousands.

By the fall of 1942, after stays ranging from weeks to six months, inmates of these camps were typically removed to one of ten more permanent American-style concentration camps. Run by the newly created War Relocation Authority (WRA), these camps were located away from the coasts, in some of the most desolate parts of California, Arizona, Idaho, Wyoming, Colorado, Utah, and Arkansas.

Because of his American citizenship and Christian religious principles, Gordon Hirabayashi believed that subjecting Japanese Americans to curfew and removal en masse was unnecessary, discriminatory, and unjust. He determined to resist both orders on principle and retained a lawyer. Gordon's decision caught the attention of progressive Seattle community leaders and organizations—including the Quakers and the American Civil Liberties Union—and his stand quickly achieved the status of a test case with support from Seattle's religious and political communities.

In order to push his case forward, Gordon decided to turn himself in and declare his intention not to report to the Wartime Civil Control Administration or go to camp. Along with his Quaker lawyer Arthur

Barnett, Gordon presented himself at the Seattle FBI office on May 13, 1942, and submitted his written statement, "Why I Refuse to Register for Evacuation."

The initial trial, *Gordon Kiyoshi Hirabayashi v. the United States of America*, was held in the U.S. district court in Seattle, with the Gordon Hirabayashi Defense Committee, made up of progressives from the University District and Seattle, providing support. Gordon was charged with violating Public Law 503, violating the curfew order, and violating Civilian Exclusion Order No. 57. Lawyer Frank Walters moved that the court dismiss the indictment on the grounds that the defendant had been deprived of liberty and property without due process of law and that Executive Order 9066, Proclamations 2 and 3, Civilian Exclusion Order 57 issued by the military commander, and Public Law 503 were all unconstitutional and void. The judge pronounced Gordon guilty of each offense charged in the two counts of the indictment. His trial lasted just one day.

The district court decision was appealed in February 1943 and then transferred to the circuit court of appeals in San Francisco, which in turn passed the case on to the U.S. Supreme Court on March 27, 1943.

Gordon and his lawyers pursued judicial review at the Supreme Court. In May 1943, the court heard Gordon's appeal, and the following month, his convictions were upheld. The justices decided to hear and rule on only the curfew aspect of the case. Ultimately, they upheld the right of the president and Congress to take any necessary measures needed to defend national security in times of crisis. Although the case generated judicial debate, on June 21, 1943, all of the Supreme Court justices ended up concurring with the majority in regard to the legality of the imposed curfew.

Almost forty years later, in January 1983, new legal teams for Fred Korematsu, Minoru Yasui, and Gordon Hirabayashi, headed by Peter Irons, appealed the rulings of the district courts where the three men were first tried. The case, *Gordon K. Hirabayashi v. United States of America*, hit the U.S. Court of Appeals of the Ninth Circuit on March 2, 1987, with an unusual legal claim: writ of error *coram nobis*. This was, in effect, a motion to vacate each of the convictions because the prosecuting attorneys had withheld critical and available information and may have thereby negatively influenced the judges' ruling.

After almost two years of attempts by prosecution lawyers to contest and delay the case, Judge Donald S. Voorhees, presiding in the U.S. district court in Seattle, where Gordon had originally been tried, issued his ruling on February 10, 1986. While Judge Voorhees determined that Gordon had been unjustly convicted for resisting incarceration, he upheld the conviction for curfew violation, opining that such measures had been justified and that, in any case, government misconduct did not invalidate the need for a curfew. Gordon and his lawyers appealed this decision, however. On September 24, 1987, Judge Mary Schroeder of the Ninth Circuit Court of Appeals, overruled Judge Voorhees, requiring him to also vacate Gordon's conviction for the curfew violation charge. Although government lawyers appealed this ruling, the court rejected the appeal at the end of 1987. Gordon's wartime conviction for defying DeWitt's curfew order was finally vacated on January 12, 1988.

There are at least three reasons to attend to *Hirabayashi v. United States* today. First, it illustrates a situation in which the system of checks and balances broke down. Instead of fully tackling the issue of mass removal and mass incarceration of an entire ethnic or racial group, the Supreme Court justices dodged a key constitutional issue by focusing only on the possible wartime need for curfew regulations.

Second, the partial success of Gordon's *coram nobis* case in 1986 demonstrated that the federal government withheld evidence from the Supreme Court in making its case. Using the government's own documentary record, Gordon's legal team was able to show that military leaders knew full well that Japanese Americans did not constitute a wholesale threat to national security. There were means available, that is, for identifying and containing those persons inside the community who may indeed have constituted a potential threat. This point would have reinforced Gordon's claim that the federal government's policies and actions violated the Fifth Amendment.

Third, as legal scholars Jerry Kang and Eric Muller have both indicated, in a post-9/11 world, the domestic use of a wholesale curfew against an identifiable segment of the U.S. population—such as Middle Eastern or Muslim Americans—is a much more likely scenario should any site in the lower forty-eight states be subject to a large-scale, violent attack. In this sense, the Supreme Court's Hirabayashi ruling could take on a new relevance, especially since the mass incarceration of a domestic population would be relatively unlikely, not only because of the expense, but also because the public at large would probably not support such a measure.

A NOTE ON METHOD

While Gordon was in good health for a man in his eighties, his memories of the 1940s had gradually faded over time. Although he wanted to write a full-length autobiography, and the University of Washington Press asked him to generate a manuscript along these lines, this was a project that he outlined but never undertook to write.

As Jim began to pore over Gordon's diaries and letters from the 1940s, it was clear that these materials, along with the many papers, speeches, and notes in his files, provided enough material to reconstruct his story from his own words. They were written at different times, however, for different occasions and for different audiences. Moreover, some versions of the stories were more detailed than others. In addition, especially in the more informal accounts in his diaries and personal letters, Gordon went back and forth between different topics, making transitions that might be difficult for readers to follow. Thus, while preserving his words as written might be important for other purposes, Jim composed the initial draft of this manuscript in the following fashion.

The book draws most heavily from Gordon's prison diaries and letters. The diaries were handwritten in spiral notebooks and cover a wide range of topics. Gordon's personal letters include more than two hundred of his own letters as well as a number of letters he received from various correspondents. Since these sources cover an enormous range of topics, in no particular chronological or thematic order, Jim made the first pass at selecting materials and putting them into a readable narrative. For example, when Gordon wrote about specific jail mates, he didn't do so in a continuous sequence; rather, inmates' portraits are intermixed with other topics in both his diaries and his letters. Similarly, we gathered the meditations in Gordon's diaries and letters into their own section, because Gordon's philosophical thoughts—whether political, religious, social, and so on—typically were interspersed with other topics that happened to come to mind as he was writing. In some cases, this meant our taking passages out of sequence and organizing them into thematic blocks.

As a second step, Jim then drew from Gordon's published and unpublished papers, speeches, and interviews, including those he had conducted as well as those taken by other scholars (for example, Roger Daniels), community documentarians (Tom Ikeda and Denshō), playwrights (Frank Chin and Jeanne Sakata), and fellow Nisei (for example, Paul Tsuneishi). Over a period of approximately two years, Jim melded these different sources with Gordon's diaries and letters. The intent was to capture Gordon's voice (as Jim knew it) as accurately and fully as possible, in order to provide readers with insight into Gordon's thoughts at the time and the understandings he developed about his own motives and experiences some years after the fact.

After Jim generated an account in Gordon's own words, Lane worked to further organize and refine it, and he and Jim passed the manuscript back and forth for many months. Following its submission to the University of Washington Press, it was largely Lane who massaged the text further in response to comments from reviewers, colleagues who read various drafts of the manuscript, and University of Washington Press editors.

In sum, because our priority was to give readers a sense of Gordon's voice and perspectives, we've based our account on his words but have also claimed editorial rights. By rearranging and lightly (and silently) editing Gordon's words, we've tried to create an engaging, accessible account that we hope will give readers insight into the dynamic, thoughtful, and deeply spiritual person that Gordon had become by his twenties.

ACKNOWLEDGMENTS

FIRST AND FOREMOST, WE THANK GORDON'S WIFE, SUSAN CAR-
nahan, and his children, Marian, Sharon, and Jay. Lorraine Bannai,
Roger Daniels, Jerry Kang, Tetsuden Kashima, Eric Muller, Jeanne
Sakata, Paul Tsuneishi, and Karen Tei Yamashita have each shared
resources with us. In Seattle, Ken House, archivist, National Archives
and Records Administration, Pacific Alaska Region, gave us helpful
guidance on Gordon's files held there. Rebecca Pixler, assistant archivist, checked holdings for us in the King County Archives in Seattle.
Lane's research assistant, Brandon Shindo, helped prepare the glossa-
ries and photos. Eri Kameyama, master's student in Asian American
Studies at the University of California, Los Angeles, and her mother,
Junko Kameyama, helped with translations, as did Kenichiro Shi-
mada. The Kameyamas also provided valuable commentary on the
photos of the Pontiac cooperative sports day and picnic. We are grateful to them all. The comments of two anonymous readers aided our
revisions.

Three colleagues deserve special mention here. University of Washington Press editor Marianne Keddington-Lang offered us detailed
comments on the entire text. Beyond the substantive and editorial
points she raised, Marianne was also the source of great encouragement and support as we worked to refine this manuscript. Similarly,
Tetsuden Kashima and Art Hansen went beyond collegial duty in
the editorial comments they gave us, and the trenchant suggestions
they offered about how to strengthen the text were much appreciated. Marilyn Trueblood, managing editor, University of Washington
Press, and Laura Iwasaki, copy editor, helped us polish the manuscript
into its final form.

Needless to say, we alone are responsible for the account that follows. We hope that it will be as interesting for you to read as we have found it to research and write.

JAH & LRH

ACRONYMS

ACLU   American Civil Liberties Union

AFSC   American Friends Service Committee

CO   conscientious objector

CPS   Civilian Public Service

CWRIC Commission on Wartime Relocation
       and Internment of Civilians

FOR   Fellowship of Reconciliation

JACL   Japanese American Citizens League

ROTC   Reserve Officer Training Corp

WRA   War Relocation Authority

WCCA   Wartime Civil Control Administration

YMCA   Young Men's Christian Association

YPPC   Young People's Christian Conference

YWCA   Young Women's Christian Association

A PRINCIPLED STAND

An Issei-Nisei Family

PART I INTRODUCES THE HIRABAYASHI FAMILY, TRACING ITS roots back to Nagano prefecture, northeast of Tokyo. As compilers of the book, we have drawn freely from Gordon's personal correspondence and a number of his published and unpublished papers covering his parents' background and his own upbringing, as well as from interviews and conversations that he had with Roger Daniels, Jeanne Sakata, Paul Tsuneishi, Tom Ikeda, and Jim Hirabayashi.

Quotes from Shungo Hirabayashi are from an extensive oral history that Jim Hirabayashi took with his father in 1971.

Religion and spirituality make up a key theme in Gordon's upbringing and youth. What is most interesting in this regard is the way that his parents' participation in Mukyōkai, a Christian sect, laid the foundations for his own spiritual beliefs, which he began to explore seriously on his own when he went off to college at the University of Washington (UW), where he became a Quaker. In this sense, it is no accident that Uchimura Kanzo, the founder of Mukyōkai, noted his strong sympathies toward the Quakers he met when he studied Christianity in the United States.

Beyond this, readers will see that while Japanese language and values were an integral part of Gordon's upbringing, so were elementary and secondary school and all-American activities such as the Boy Scouts. It was in the Scouts, incidentally, that Gordon had his first real brush with race and racialization, at the tender age of eleven. Experiences along these lines enabled him to be surprisingly mature when he faced discrimination at the university level and found his mentors caught between their ideals and the racial color line they adhered to in their daily lives.

Shungo Hirabayashi, with kith and kin, shortly before leaving for the United States, Nagano prefecture, Japan, ca. 1907. From left, seated: Motoyoshi Hirabayashi, Shungo Hirabayashi, and Toshiharu Hirabayashi. Standing, at far right, is Takashi Tojo, a close family friend. Courtesy of James A. Hirabayashi

Shungo Hirabayashi, Seattle, 1910. To the left of the photograph, under the paper frame, he had written in Japanese: "Dear Parents: As a memorial to my third anniversary in the U.S. 1910, March 22nd. Hirabayashi Shungo." Courtesy of Sharon M. Yuen

Shungo Hirabayashi (*left*), next to Hamao Hirabayashi, Toshimaru Hirabayashi, and Fukashi Kiyosawa, Seattle, ca. 1907–8. They are already dressed in Western-style suits. Courtesy of James A. Hirabayashi

Shungo Hirabayashi, Seattle, ca. 1912. Courtesy of James A. Hirabayashi

Mitsuko Sawada poses for a portrait in Nagano prefecture, Japan, ca. 1913. Note the Gibson girl hairstyle. Courtesy of Susan Carnahan

Mitsuko Sawada (*third row, second from left*) with fellow students, all "picture brides," Hotaka, Nagano prefecture, Japan, ca. 1913. Iguchi Sensei (*fourth row, third from left*), a disciple of Uchimura Kanzo's, was the director of the Kensei Academy, where Sawada studied Christianity and English in preparation for emigrating to the United States. Courtesy of James A. Hirabayashi

Mitsuko Hirabayashi in formal wedding dress, Seattle, ca. 1914. Courtesy of James A. Hirabayashi

Shungo and Mitsuko Hirabayashi, Seattle, date unknown. Courtesy of James A. Hirabayashi

CHAPTER 1

Hotaka to Seattle

MY DAD, SHUNGO, CAME FROM HOTAKA, A TOWN IN THE FOOT-
hills of the Japanese Alps in Nagano prefecture. There was a neighborhood of a dozen Hirabayashi households in a rural setting at the edge
of town. He was the eldest son in one of the Hirabayashi households.
His father was a clerk in the town office, and his mother tended what
was left of their farm, a few small rice paddies. It was the beginning
of the twentieth century, and it was hard times for the peasantry.
In order to underwrite industrialization, as Japan began competing
with the colonizing Western powers, the Meiji government imposed
heavy taxes on farms and other property. Even as a teenager, Dad
wondered about his future: "My prospects are not good."

With the military victories in the Sino-Japanese War of 1894 and
the Russo-Japanese War of 1904, the prestige of the samurai tradition
was transferred onto the modern military forces. Dad was inspired by
this militaristic spirit:

> Among the youth everyone wanted to join the army, and I went to
> the village office to enlist, but I was told that I was not old enough
> and was rejected. Wondering what I should do, I heard about a man
> who went to America and made a fortune in five years. Then came
> the recruiters for overseas work, and they said, "If you want to go
> to America, learn English and Christianity." Before hearing about
> America, I did not want to go there because Christianity was associ-
> ated with America, and I was against foreign religions. I had even

Nagano Prefecture

Town of Matsumoto

Honshu

Tokyo

Japan

1000KM

Nagano Prefecture, Japan. Hotaka, the hometown
of Shungo Hirabayashi, is near Matsumoto.

gone once with my school friends to harass the missionaries who had come to evangelize in the neighboring town.

I wanted to go to America, so I went to the house of Iguchi Kikenji, principal of Kensei Academy, to hear him speak. He talked about the Scriptures, "Christianity is to love people. Love other people as you love yourself. If you are hit on the right cheek, turn your left cheek." Principal Iguchi argued that violence and war were not the solution to conflict. I was convinced—if Christianity is this way, it is very good.

Iguchi was a disciple of Uchimura Kanzo, the founder of Mukyōkai, a non-church Christian sect in Japan, an unusual Japanese religious denomination. Uchimura had enrolled at the newly established Sapporo Agricultural College in 1877. William Clark, president of Massachusetts Agricultural College, arrived in 1876 to help set up the college. While there, he formed a group, Believers in Jesus Christ, that included all of the first-year students. Uchimura enrolled in 1877 and, pressured by his cohort, joined the student Christian group too.

Uchimura traveled to America in 1884 and visited the Quakers in Pennsylvania who had contributed to his theological perspectives in Japan. He said of Quaker Mary Morris: "I was conscious that she was a partner in my Christian works. She often told me that 'thee is almost a Quaker theeself.' I was always sorry that I was 'almost' and not 'entirely.' Still . . . my critics recognized in me a strong Quaker influence, and that influence was Mary Morris of Overbrook, Philadelphia." Uchimura then attended Amherst College in Massachusetts and came under the influence of President Julius H. Seelye: "He opened my eyes to the evangelical truth in Christianity," he said.

After a semester at Hartford Theological Seminary in Connecticut, Uchimura returned to Japan in 1888. Reacting negatively to the materialistic orientation of Western Christianity, Uchimura rejected the rituals, priestly hierarchy, dogmas, and liturgy of the traditional Christian church. Instead, he emphasized a personal experience with God and a morality based on truth, hard work, and responsibility to others. On this basis, Uchimura founded Mukyōkai, the non-church

Christian movement, by establishing small intimate fellowships where the members shared the responsibility of exercising their faith.

Iguchi, a disciple of Uchimura's, established Kensei Academy in 1898 in Nagano prefecture. The curriculum included Bible study, English, ethics, Chinese language, Confucius, Mencius, and public policy. Boys and girls were not segregated but taught in one room. There was a synthesis of the genuine spiritual traditions of Japan with the Christian gospel as interpreted in the Puritan manner for the betterment of society. Although the government encouraged immigration by urging the young to go to another country to earn money and come back, Iguchi encouraged his students differently. "Have good ambition. Don't go to USA just to make money. Do not be a slave to materialism but go there to build God's kingdom. Live a courageous life. Be a good citizen. Christianity is to love people—love other people as you love yourself. If you strongly have that spirit, there will be no trouble in this world."

Dad, responding to this very positively, said, "I thought that if Christianity is this way, it is very good. I became convinced, and my heart was changed. With this Christian spirit I came to America, and I have kept that faith all my life."

SHINKOKYO: THE NEW HOMELAND

My dad and his Issei associates were mostly young single males from the rural peasantry, the majority of whom had at least an elementary school education. They came as *dekasegi*, temporary migrants, with the intention of returning to Japan in a few years—rich! This aspiration shifted as gold was not found on the streets. The Gentlemen's Agreement, 1907–8, curtailed Japanese migration to America. Only families of the Issei were allowed to migrate, which led to the development of the "picture bride" custom. The Issei sent for wives and established families, and communities emerged as they began their process of integrating into American society.

Confronted with legal restrictions and general racism, the strong sense of group and communality sustained social protection for the

Issei. The tendency toward self-effacement and deference generally was misunderstood by Westerners, who felt that if the Issei thought so little of themselves, they were unworthy of respect. In other circumstances, misunderstanding had produced stereotypes of Japanese as being "sly, inscrutable, untrustworthy, and suspicious." Two major anti-Japanese arguments were that they presented a "threat against the standard of living" and they were "unassimilable." That they were not from upper-class origins in Japan may have made it easier for the Issei to accept race discrimination and low status with a measure of fatalism. Japanese traits, in other words, facilitated knowing one's place, doing what is expected, and having the perseverance to survive. In this sense, defense mechanisms for coping with second-class treatment were an Issei adaptive characteristic on the U.S. mainland.

Dad left Japan from Yokohama in 1907.

> My dream to go to America came true. Five of us cousins left our families and neighborhood and migrated to America. Initially, we got jobs on the railroad—two teams of four on a handcar. Almost a year later, one of the fellows wanted to run up ahead to see if trains were coming. He jumped off in front of the handcar and was run over. The car cut him in half. After that, none of us went back to work on the railroad. We all took various jobs in Seattle.

A Mukyōkai fellowship group was formed as soon as they settled, and Iguchi Sensei sent many letters and Christian magazines and materials to his former students from Kensei Academy. The Issei from the same town formed the Hotaka Club in Seattle. They also belonged to the Nagano Prefectural Association, a social and mutual aid group, as well as the Nihonjinkai, or Japanese Association, which included all Issei in the Seattle area.

In 1911, several cousins of Dad's, along with friends from Nagano prefecture, formed a collective and began a vegetable garden in Pontiac, on the shore of Lake Washington. Later, this area became part of the Sand Point Naval Air Base. After they brought the harvest in, they hauled vegetables by horse and wagon to the Pike Place Market on the Seattle waterfront. They sponsored picnic gatherings, with food and games, and even invited Caucasian acquaintances who lived in the area to join them. Dad thought of starting a family.

I did not go back to Japan to find a wife but searched for my future wife through my relatives. I trusted everything to my parents. After the families made the arrangements, Mitsu went over to my parents' home, attended Kensei Academy to learn English, and then came to join me in 1914. My family found a real good match for me, so I made a commitment to marry Suzawa Mitsuko. I feel filled with hope for my bright future. We registered as husband and wife in Hotaka, and the following year Mitsu landed in the USA. We had a marriage ceremony in Seattle.

In 1919, four families of the Pontiac collective, including two Hirabayashi families—my father's family and the Toshiharu Hirabayashi family—moved to Thomas, Washington, a rural community twenty miles south of Seattle. These families formed a Christian cooperative, White River Garden, and purchased forty acres of land. Then the difficult development process began: clearing the land of stumps, digging ditches for better drainage, fertilizing the soil, cultivating, and building their homes.

In the early 1920s, John Isao Nishinoiri, a graduate student from Japan, was engaged in field research on Japanese farms on the outskirts of Seattle for his master's degree in sociology at the University of Washington. Nishinoiri wrote:

About five miles south of Kent on the west road leading to Auburn stand four neatly painted houses—this is the White River Garden—they came from the same district in Japan, Azumi in Nagano prefecture. Although four different families live there, they plant, crop, buy, and sell together. Machinery, tools, barns, horses, and all equipment are owned and used in common. Cooperation is not a theory with them; it is a daily practice. This occupational cooperation finds its source in their spiritual cooperation acquired in Japan under the influence of a non-denominational evangelist . . . [and] binds them together closely.

In spite of the overwhelming materialism of modern American civilization, they maintain their simple Christian faith in its Puritan form. They do not work on Sunday, even in the busiest seasons, and never fail to meet for the purpose of worshipping God. They have no minister, so each of them speaks in turn of his thoughts and experiences. Their simple service is opened and closed with hymns and prayer, and when I attended I felt as if I were sitting with the Puritans of the colonial period.

In Washington State, the 1923 Alien Land Law prevented noncitizens from owning land. Before 1952, immigrant Issei were ineligible for naturalization, so the White River Garden property was purchased in the name of the oldest Nisei in our group, Aiko Katsuno, who was then ten years old. Since she was a minor, they appointed Mrs. Nora Murphy, the wife of Rev. U. G. Murphy, a former missionary in Japan, as her legal guardian. Once the government officials found out about this arrangement, the state of Washington filed suit against White River Garden Corporation, even though it was properly registered in a citizen's name. Government lawyers claimed that the purchase of White River Garden was a deceit and a subterfuge insofar as the real owners of the property were the alien parents.

Unlike others facing similar charges, the Katsunos and Hirabayashis, who developed White River Garden, fought the state and appealed their case to the state supreme court. We lost at each stage, until finally the White River Garden land was taken by the state of Washington. Our families were forced to lease the fields they had formerly owned from the state, in order to continue farming there!

I was a young child then and did not know what was going on, except remembering concerned looks and worries during the *komban saiban no sodankai*, or evening discussion meetings, on the progress of the court case. There were many late nights like that, which followed a full day's work in the field. There was something that gave strength and meaning to the Mukyokai cooperative members. Their collective belief in the justice of their cause motivated them to confront the state in fighting for what they felt was right. It was also a reflection of the faith they had in God and the genuine fellowship they enjoyed as a group. Something of the spirit demonstrated in their day-to-day living was like a seed in my developing personality and character. The model that these Christian pioneers demonstrated for me must surely have been the source of strength and the guiding light that helped me to confront the government at the time of World War II.

Several Hirabayashi families were part of the Issei Pontiac cooperative farm group, Pontiac, Washington, ca. 1910–12. *From left*: Shungo Hirabayashi, Toshiharu Hirabayashi, unidentified friend, and Motoyoshi Hirabayashi. American flags are visible on the beams of the front porch, an open display of the group's orientation. Courtesy of James A. Hirabayashi

Members of the Pontiac cooperative farm group, Pontiac, Washington, ca. 1912–14. Seated in the front row is Mrs. S. Katsuno (*third from left*), holding her infant, Aiko Katsuno. In the second row, standing, is Takashi Tojo (*left*), S. Katsuno (*third from left*), and Toshiharu Hirabayashi (*fourth from left*). Shungo Hirabayashi is in the third row, standing, at left. The Katsunos and Hirabayashis lost their White River Garden land to the state of Washington by escheat in 1921. They took their case to the state supreme court but lost their appeal. Courtesy of James A. Hirabayashi

Japanese and Euro-American women bobbing for apples at the Pontiac cooperative farm group's sports day and picnic, Pontiac, Washington, April 26, 1914. The Issei invited Euro-American families in the neighborhood to participate in these festivities. Courtesy of Jay Hirabayashi

Issei members of the Pontiac cooperative farm group and their families, Pontiac, Washington, ca. 1912–14. The adults were from either Hotaka or Nagano prefecture, Japan. In the front row, seated are Aiko Katsuno (*second from left*) and her mother, Mrs. S. Katsuno (*third from left*). Standing in the second row, left side: Mitsu Hirabayashi (*fourth from left*); third row, Takashi Tojo and Shungo Hirabayashi (*fourth and fifth from left*); back row: Mr. Katsuno (seventh from left). Courtesy of James Hirabayashi

Shungo Hirabayashi outside his new, self-constructed farmhouse, White River Garden cooperative, Thomas, Washington, ca. 1919–20. The families who lived and worked on White River Garden, including the Hirabayashi and Katsuno families, were members of Mukyokai, the non-church Christian movement founded by Uchimura Kanzo. Courtesy of James Hirabayashi

Mitsuko Hirabayashi holding an infant Gordon.

The Hirabayashi family during the Great Depression, Thomas, Washington, 1934. Front row, from left: Mitsuko; Richard, age three; James, age eight; and Toshiko (Esther), age five. Second row: Gordon, age sixteen; Shungo; and Edward, age eleven. Courtesy of Esther Hirabayashi

CHAPTER 2

Growing Up in America

I WAS BORN IN 1918 IN SEATTLE, THE SECOND SON. AFTER WE moved to our Thomas farm in 1919, my brother Paul, who was two years older, had an accident while riding on his bicycle. The medical care in those days was not good, and Paul died from damage to his kidneys. I then became the *chonan*—eldest son—destined to be the family heir, and received special training. "It's your responsibility," I was told. My parents bonded me to the role of *chonan* and all the trappings that went with it, so my socialization really differed from that of my younger siblings. Dad said:

> I am a farmer's son. I didn't become a farmer because I had no
> choice. It really fits my personality and my constitution. Oh, coun-
> tryside life: if there is a holy project in this world, agriculture is
> one of them. In this quiet, serene, wonderful environment, I can
> do my best from the bottom of my heart. I consider agriculture my
> vocation in life and I feel very happy about that. The success of the
> project is beyond our control. It is up to God's power and guidance.

The thing about Dad that saved him from being a narrow religious bigot was that he farmed to see things grow from tiny plants into lovely vegetables. He once told me, "They are alive and I can see them growing." It was as much a creative act as any artist's, for he loved the aesthetics—the beauty of it—as much as being a farmer. Even though he never earned much money through the Depression, we always had enough to eat. Truck gardening was seen as security in subsistence. You work diligently and hard for your gains. I was seeing, so far as his faith and practice were concerned, action with great integrity.

Dad was forthright, but he wasn't a good businessman because he was too honest. He wouldn't cheat anybody. I remember we used to get so exasperated at Dad's *baka-shojiki*—being honest to a ridiculous extent. Dad would insist on packing lettuce with good, beautiful ones in the bottom and middle, not just saved for the top layer. Our plea that nobody else was that stupid, and that that kind of honesty was not expected in business, made no impression on Dad. He would respond, "Honesty is honesty—besides I have to live with myself."

My mother definitely was a frustrated farmer's wife. She always worked incredibly hard and did all the household chores but intensely disliked the farm. To her, all the never-ending hard labor from morning till night was tedious, and there was very little money to show for it.

The main thing about my mom was her spirit of determination. During the Depression, she decided that she wanted to have one of those foot-treadle Singer sewing machines. It was very expensive, but this didn't stop Mom. She marched down to the Singer Company and asked the salesperson what she could do, short of paying, to get the machine she wanted. The salesperson said if she could get five other women to come in and purchase Singers, the company would give Mom her own machine in return. So in the heart of the Depression, Mom went out and somehow managed to do just that. That's why I say that once she put her mind to something, she was very focused.

She played the piano—she was a farmer's wife, but I guess she got interested in it. Mom had an opportunity and bought an old-style square grand. Ours was the only farm home that had any kind of piano. Mom learned to play it from a high school girl: "I have a piano; I want to learn to play it. Teach me!" Mom learned primarily hymns and folk songs, like Stephen Foster tunes.

Mom also liked to read books and journals. One of the magazines that came from Japan regularly was *Shufu no Tomo*, or *Housewife's Friend*. She used to contribute some articles and poetry now and then, incognito, signing her pieces "A Farmer's Wife." The neighboring farming wives said, "Hey! I just read this. Did you write this? It sounds just like you!" So the neighbors suspected Mom, but she acted naive about it. "Oh no, that wasn't me." Under other circumstances, she would have been a magazine editor or something of that nature.

She even got into politics in the Issei community. She was vice president of the local Japanese association for a couple of terms. That organization was male dominated, and women had no franchise—they weren't eligible to vote. A leadership role was quite unusual for a female. I think if Mom were male she would have been president, but even vice president was unusual. She was fairly lucid, and this was in a generally chauvinistic community. She was smart, though. If Mom had a strategy to present, she would do it as "something my husband and I discussed." She used the male voice, since if a woman puts an idea forward, it gets squashed right away. So that's part of the speech etiquette—a part of manipulating reality. If a woman wanted to get an idea across, she didn't present it as "I, a woman." She would quote a male neighbor, or the husband, or act as though various other males had proposed it to begin with and that she was just endorsing their idea.

To an outside observer, it would seem as if my mother made all of the decisions. She was the articulate one, publicly. Dad didn't try to dominate. Mom excelled in her oral articulations—he supplied calmness. My father was the quiet and solid foundation, with his unostentatious dedication to the oneness of belief and practice. My mother was the fire, providing warmth and sometimes intense heat. She was an activist, outgoing, articulate, and feisty. This, by the way, was such a contrast to the norms of conduct in the Japanese community. There, the mottos were sayings like "Don't rock the boat" and "Don't do anything to attract attention, for right or wrong; you'll suffer for it." So Mom was the fire; fire produces light. Dad was the anchor, the Rock of Ages, complementing the light. My brother Ed once said:

> I think we had a pretty easy-going fundamentalist Christian home. Moral behavior, certain clear-cut values in life, were not questioned

but followed. No alcohol, no card playing, perfect attendance at Sunday school, but we never felt uptight about it. The greatest moral and spiritual impact came from my parents' way of life. Their living example had to do with honesty and integrity in all aspects of human relations.

GROWING UP NISEI: SECOND GENERATION

In the prewar rural communities on the West Coast, the cultural heritage of the Nisei children was strongly influenced by their Japanese parents. The Issei generally encouraged the Nisei to value the same principles that their parents grew up with. I did not learn to speak English until I began elementary school. Japanese was spoken in the home, in our social circles, and during community affairs. Not only the food but many customs and important values instilled in us as part of growing up were Japanese. The Issei emphasized group centeredness, relatively downgrading the individual. Emerging from this would be concepts like *on*, a strong feeling of social obligation; *giri*, a sense of duty to the group to which one belongs; *ninjo*, a sense of sympathy and compassion for others. Associated with the above concepts was a tendency toward understatement. The by-products of these concepts and emphases were *otonashii*, or reserve; *enryo*, deference; and *shikataganai*, or acceptance of reality. The Issei said, "Face is important—keep a proper face! Be respectful and decent." Within the Issei social context, these patterns are meaningfully integrated. The Issei brought some of these basic Japanese characteristics with them, but Issei necessarily adjusted cultural patterns, too, in the building of a new community in the American setting.

In our community, the Nihonjinkai, the Japanese Association, sponsored gatherings during holidays, the emperor's birthday, and other events. They also established a Japanese-language school. I wanted to go because all of my friends were going. And after class, I still had another hour to play baseball. If I came right home, I would have had to do chores, so I went a couple of blocks around the corner from our grade school. There were two classes at the Nihonjinkai building. They had a Nisei educated in Japan (Kibei), who went to the regular school with us. He was ahead of me in the upper grades. He taught us Japanese, but he had a rough time because we made it hard on him. The principal, Mr. Okimoto, lived upstairs.

I attended the local grade school. We were in double grades, and the principal, Mr. Fergin, taught seventh and eighth grades—history, geography, spelling, sometimes literature, reading. He did the whole class. And then arithmetic, and I can't remember what else, but there were certain things that were done separately. I could hear them, and because of that I learned to do it. Then Mr. Fergin told us, "We're doing the state exam, and if any of you would like to take additional tests now, you won't have to do them next year." Most of us decided to take this offer. I passed half of the eighth-grade tests. Fergin said, "You passed these and did just as well as the eighth graders. Why don't you try the rest of them?" I took them, passed, and was able to graduate. So I finished grade school a year early, but I was socially pretty immature. I started high school when I was twelve and a half!

About half of my grade-school classmates were Japanese. When I went to high school in Auburn, the proportion of Japanese dropped, but we were still a large visible minority—the only minority in the valley. In school, we participated in various activities, especially sports and other groups as well, but our numbers were not large. I participated in the glee club, language club, operetta, theater, and Hi-Y (High School Young Men's Christian Association) and was a sports editor of the school paper. I made the honor roll consistently.

An important part of my teen years was participation in the local Japanese American social clubs, religious fellowship groups, Japanese American Christian conferences, and Nisei sports and church leagues. I subscribed to the Nisei *Courier* newspaper [James Sakamoto's *Japanese-American Courier*] to keep up on community affairs. Through the Boy Scouts leaders' conferences, I learned to participate in interethnic circles beyond my high school environment. It was kind of a springboard for my inclination to take first-class citizenship seriously in spite of the knowledge of second-class status of Japanese in the prewar days.

RELIGIOUS EXPERIENCE: CHRISTIANITY

I got religious training very early. The Issei families in the White River Garden cooperative conducted Mukyōkai services in their homes. They met without formal preaching or leaders and primarily discussed their religious principles and beliefs.

My father instilled in me the importance of having convictions and adhering to the standard of conduct dictated by those convictions. Proper etiquette based on Christian principles was part of critical behavior control. What's good: truth! I got quite a bit of Uchimura Kanzo's principles, but I didn't get it from my parents drilling it into me. When I visited Japan in the 1990s, a news reporter, Miyabara Yasuharu, said, "I never expected to hear Gordon Hirabayashi mention Uchimura Kanzo, nor Iguchi Kikenji, and I came to realize what Iguchi taught the immigrants in Kensei Academy was later carried out by the second-generation Nisei in the USA." Since both of my parents were influenced by this unique Christian movement in Japan, this background led to my eventual contact with and membership in the Quakers (Society of Friends) during my university days.

An occasional pastor who came down to our area was the Reverend U. G. Murphy, a Methodist minister from Seattle. Once a missionary to Japan, he came once a month to meet with the Mukyōkai group. With the aid of Reverend Murphy, the group formed a relationship with the local Christians and established the Thomas Union Church. The Stewart family, Pentecostal fundamentalists, were the anchors of the church. Two brothers, John and James, had kids in my school classes. They were the mainstay of the church, and their standing got us the use of the Thomas School auditorium for services, which was probably a violation of the law. We drove over in our trucks, and there was a hymn service. We also met in our own little groups. The church did the Bible stuff and contests for the kids. I got a New Testament for memorizing all the books of the Bible. It took me until high school to kick the fundamentalists out of my life. I just couldn't take it anymore. I mean, I just decided it doesn't make sense; I can't go anymore. So I didn't go to Sunday school after that. But I didn't reject religion.

There were various Christian denominations in the area. I knew about the Baptists because they had the scout troop there, a Nisei scout troop, with Reverend Andrews as the scoutmaster. I knew about those other denominations, but my parents said they didn't belong to those groups. They believed in Christianity as Christianity, not divided into pieces like that. That's what Uchimura felt, too. There were appeals and efforts made by Seattle and Tacoma churches because the Mukyōkai group was known as a unique group. At that time, they resisted joining other denominations, but they went to some general meetings and were respected by all.

I joined the Boy Scouts when I was eleven and in the fifth grade. The scoutmaster, Mr. Bechtol, was my grade-school teacher. He organized our troop, and we got the troop number 453. Henry Tsuchiya, a Nisei who was about to become an Eagle Scout, was one of the leaders. We got into a little racial war. Mr. Bechtol said, "I'm going to delegate some responsibility to some of you. The most experienced person here is Henry, so he is the most likely one to be the senior patrol leader." There was protest, however, against this idea. Obviously, Henry was the star and experienced, whereas the oldest of the Jarvis brothers was already in high school but a beginner in scouts. I think the parents protested, "Why is this Jap becoming the senior leader?" Bechtol had to step back. What he did was he named Jarvis the senior patrol leader but kept Henry as his junior assistant scoutmaster. I never became an Eagle because I never had time to go camping and that sort of thing—anything that cost money. We didn't have much cash.

The Auburn Christian Fellowship (ACF) was an interdenominational coalition of Nisei Christians in the Auburn area. The Issei probably organized it, but we Nisei ran it. ACF members attended the Salvation Army summer camp. I became one of the leaders. I also attended the Young People's Christian Conferences (YPCC).

In the 1935 Auburn High School annual, I am pictured in the Young Men's Christian Association (YMCA) photograph. Auburn's Hi-Y was affiliated with the National YMCA. The purpose of the club is expressed in the slogan "To create, maintain, and extend throughout the school and community high standards of Christian character." Hi-Y is like a social club, but we had religious aspects. There were two Japanese members, myself and Takuzo Tsuchiya. I brought him in. It's a white man's club, you know.

On the other side of Thomas, the Japanese Americans were mainly Buddhist. We looked on the people who went to Buddhist temple as misguided, but my friends who were in Boy Scouts and all, they came to our Sunday school. One of them, Koji Horiuchi, was sent to a sanitarium. Some Catholic guy came around and made him a Catholic without contacting the parents, and after he died, we found out that they had control of the funeral. They talked to his parents, who asked for our support. So Mom and Dad represented them and said that this is not the best way to do it, and they worked out a compromise service. As his closest friend, I was asked to say a few words. I wore my scout uniform. Our scoutmaster came and said something, and I said something, and that was the first public speech I made.

BICULTURAL NORMS

Beginning in elementary school, the teacher would encourage me by saying, "Speak up. What do you think?" The restraint from the Japanese value system lay heavily on my shoulders, telling me not to blurt out something. I frequently sat in class like a sphinx.

We Nisei are a peculiar people. We adapted to two Americas, coping with and minimizing one in order to preserve the other, to which we had subscribed wholeheartedly. We put together the kind of qualities and values from our bicultural background that would help us survive the problems we had to confront. While we made our choice and identified with American values, we were not fully accepted.

There was the duality of the cross-cultural norms of the Japanese vis-à-vis the North American ways and values. Simultaneously, we also had to grapple with the inconsistency of North American ideals versus practices as experienced in the state of Washington. While being native-born American citizens, we faced many restrictions, as there were overt double standards in regard to democracy and racism. In civics classes I was exposed to American ideals to which I subscribed wholeheartedly—ideals such as all persons are created equal, with liberty and justice for all, equal protection under the law, and citizenship regardless of race, religion, creed, or national origins. Before World War II, human rights laws were nonexistent. Conduct of the form "white gentiles only," referring to the better residential areas, was considered a private contract and, therefore, was legal. Real estate contracts, which had what were commonly known as "restrictive covenants," included words like "When you sell your home, it must be to a white gentile only." And there were no minorities, in terms of schoolteachers, professional engineers, civil servants. The "better" restaurants and hotels excluded minorities. Everything from public swimming pools to private clubs allowed minorities in only through the service entrance.

My parents insisted on general ethical training, but one of the weaknesses of parental control in our situation was that as we became more assimilated, our ability to communicate effectively with our parents began to weaken. I was wondering about that, but actually it turned out not to be so much of a factor. A good portion of the influence of my parents didn't come from their lecturing me and disciplining me. Their example was in the way they lived—their behavior. If Dad said he was going to do something, everyone would believe him because they trusted him. It was the kind of thing I was aware of, and was made aware of in other ways. You know, there is one basic principle of truth: if it's valid on Sunday, it's valid on Monday, too. So I was given that message, one way or another. My parents' teaching came by way of their doing it, so language wasn't a factor that interfered that much.

When I would express my views at home, a great family crisis often occurred as my parents wondered out loud how I could ignore the priority of family values by insisting on my own. Moreover, because the Japanese were clearly second class, I wanted to escape the disadvantages by shunning Japanese language and many of the cultural patterns that were visibly "exotic" and "peculiar." I feel my experiences are very common to the Nisei as a whole. There was a strong identification with American culture and values on the part of the Nisei, with Japanese culture and values definitely being of lower priority if not clearly rejected. But the Nisei confronted another major obstacle in their socialization. While the majority had made their choice and identified with American values (the preamble, the flag salute, the Bill of Rights, and the Constitution), the Nisei were never accepted fully. Although they were native-born American citizens, there were many restrictions.

How did Nisei cope with such inconsistencies? The Japanese heritage, modified in America, together with the climate of racism worked in peculiar ways to produce a special nonconfrontational posture. There is a Japanese proverb that describes these characteristics well: *Deru kugi wa utareru* (The nail that sticks out is the one that gets hit). So don't rock the boat. Bend with the wind. Do not draw attention to yourself, for that could only end to your disadvantage. Confronting injustice, therefore, does not enter one's mind as a possibility. Survival is the major objective.

As a Nisei growing up in America, I was increasingly incorporating Western values, goals, and styles into my life. My early Japanese values—hard work, modesty, delaying gratification—would be adapted in interesting ways to strengthen the achievement of my increasingly Western goals. Moreover, the group approval I had begun to seek was that of the non-Japanese circles where my success more and more was being measured by achievements in school, work and play circles, and the community at large.

So I began to tell myself that first-class citizenship was a viable objective. I chose this to be a reality that I could live for. I realized that I might not immediately get it, but I could live for it. Now if I'm going to keep that with some integrity, I've got to say that rejection was something that might happen, but things are going to change. And I'm not going to accept second-class treatment, and I'm going to try to live like an American, regardless.

Gordon Hirabayashi (*front row, right*) and classmates, as shown in the *Invador*, the Auburn High School yearbook, 1934. The Hi-Y Club was a high school social and civic organization tied to the International Young Men's Christian Association. Courtesy of Louise Norikane

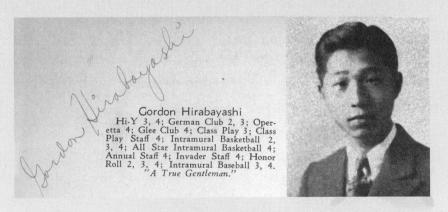

Gordon Hirabayashi
Hi-Y 3, 4; German Club 2, 3; Oper-
etta 4; Glee Club 4; Class Play 3; Class
Play Staff 4; Intramural Basketball 2,
3, 4; All Star Intramural Basketball 4;
Annual Staff 4; Invader Staff 4; Honor
Roll 2, 3, 4; Intramural Baseball 3, 4.
"A True Gentleman."

Gordon Hirabayashi's senior class photo and list of high school accomplish-
ments, *Invador*, 1935. The signature by the photograph is Gordon's, as the
yearbook was given to the family by one of his classmates. Courtesy of
Louise Norikane

Gordon Hirabayashi, age seventeen, in his Boy Scout uniform. The caption, written in Japanese on the back, reads: "As a memorial to attending a Captains' Conference of North West Squad, U.S. Boy Scouts, Thanksgiving Day, November, 1935." Courtesy of Sharon M. Yuen

Gordon Hirabayashi, college freshman, age eighteen. Taken at the Young People's Christian Conference, Seattle, November 29, 1936. Courtesy of Sharon M. Yuen

Gordon Hirabayashi at the University of Washington, ca. 1936–40. Courtesy of Jay Hirabayashi

Gordon Hirabayashi and his YMCA colleagues on a road trip in Portland, Oregon, 1940. From left: Jim Martin, Gordon Hirabayashi, Bob McFarland, Bob Rolfsness, and Howard Scott, one of Gordon's best friends. Courtesy of Susan Carnahan

Gordon Hirabayashi and Jim Martin on the road, outside of Walker, Oregon, 1940. Courtesy of Susan Carnahan

Gordon Hirabayashi (*second row, third from left*) and his colleagues at the President's Summer School, Columbia University, New York, 1940. Participation in activities such as this gave Gordon tremendous exposure to prominent leaders of the U.S. peace and pacifist social movement. Courtesy of Susan Carnahan

Gordon Hirabayashi's draft registration card (*front and back*), dated October 16, 1940. On the front of the card, on the left-hand side, Gordon wrote "I am a conscientious objector." Courtesy of the National Archives and Records Administration, Pacific Northwest Branch, Seattle, Washington

Gordon Hirabayashi, upper-division student at the University of Washington, ca. 1941. Courtesy of Susan Carnahan

Gordon Hirabayashi with William (Bill) Schmoe, Esther Schmoe's younger brother, 1941. Courtesy of Susan Carnahan

CHAPTER 3

"You're Going to College"

PURSUING AN EDUCATION WAS AN AUTOMATIC FOR ME AS LONG as I could make the grade. Although we were a poor farm family, my parents led me to anticipate university following high school, much as we were expected to move on to high school after elementary school. Mom said, "You're going to college but you are going to a good school. The guys going to the University of Washington—that's just a farm school. You're going to a school like Yale or Harvard!" She had big dreams, and she just hated the farm, so I hated it, too. I was just barely seventeen when I graduated from Auburn High School. Money was scarce in the depth of Depression, so I worked two years before entering university in 1937. I was a naive farm kid.

COMING OF AGE

The University of Washington had a quarter system, so the first couple of years I spent two quarters in class, then left and worked for two quarters. I discovered that there were a lot of things that went on during the spring term, so in 1939 I worked out a program where I went the full school year but on a part-time basis because of work. I worked in a doctor's home as a schoolboy.

When I entered UW, my one objective was to train myself so I would be a success. Success in those days was measured largely along financial lines. I thought perhaps I would be an economics major. My first quarter, along with econ, I took math. That was my first change.

As it turned out, I positively loathed Econ I, but I took quite a liking to math. I became a math major, with the intention of going into research or creating a few more theorems and analyses to frustrate future students. Math led to statistics, statistics to social statistics, social statistics to straight sociology.

If self-identity emerges from our social contacts, then the social contacts that we treasure are our reference groups. I treasured my parents and, at UW, the university groups. I belonged to the Japanese Students Club and participated in quite a few of their activities for a couple of years. As my university coursework and YMCA responsibilities became heavier, my activities with the Japanese Students Club became spotty. I actually feel this had a bearing on my awareness and preparation to challenge certain kinds of inequities, including the curfew and exclusion orders. In the broader university setting, we faced and challenged issues on their merits. In this fashion, I learned to confront issues as a citizen, not just as a minority.

On the whole, I guess you could say that I majored in extracurricular activities. That was my major interest. I got interested in various kinds of activities, and these stimulated my whole academic career. While studying my major field of sociology, the motivation was how it applied to my life, so I really majored in the sociology of life. I was also getting involved in Y activities and liking it. The personalities I met there and the kind of thrill the work there gave me just made sociology that much more a part of me. I also began to think of my future in relation to the student Christian movement. How much I wanted to get into that field! No longer did financial success mean security to me. No longer did winning economic advantages mean as much as developing true friendships. Early in my university days, I met the Quakers. And the Quakers, of course, led to my affiliation with the American Friends Service Committee [AFSC].

At the University of Washington, the YMCA was not just a religious organization. It was the center of the "independents," in contrast to the Greeks, with their racist restrictions. In my YMCA dormitory, there were about fifteen of us, largely Americans from various states but a few internationals: a couple of Chinese, a Filipino, some Canadians, and a couple of liberal Jews. There were no blacks, and I was the only person of Japanese ancestry. When issues came up, we would get into debates over certain positions. I got invested in that sort of thing. I was representing a principle in terms of debating racist restrictions at the fraternities and sororities. The Greeks weren't in line with the basic principles that are expressed in the ideal society as described in the Constitution, the Bill of Rights, and the growing number of amendments. So the opportunities that an independent place like the YMCA offered gave us a chance to intermingle and contribute to a democratic way of living.

One of my very good friends, Howard Scott, also an independent Christian, said, "You know, you're the closest person I have." He was like a brother, and we eventually became roommates. He became the freshman YMCA president, and I was on the cabinet. When he was the senior president, I became the vice president. I would have become a president in terms of the way we were doing things. We elected the cabinet, and then the cabinet elected the president. I would have been a shoo-in. At that point, they made it into an election, and during the election, I got aced out. I was shocked but I denied it. And Howard had to tell me, "I know you're hurt." Director Woodbury was shocked, too. I became the chairman of the senior cabinet, usually the president's job. So I was like the elected president, but I never challenged the president, authoritatively.

M. D. Woodbury came from Texas to become the YMCA director and was very supportive. I moved into an attic room in his house until something else opened up. That's the kind of personal support that he gave me. He allowed me to tend the Y's furnace in exchange for my YMCA room, and he brought various opportunities to my attention when they arose. On the YMCA board there were liberals like history professor Giovanni Costigan; engineering professor Frederick B. Farquharson and his wife, Washington senator Mary Farquharson; the Reverend Ray Roberts, a former YMCA director in China; and Quaker lawyer Arthur Barnett, whose wife, Virginia Barnett, was the assistant director of the University YWCA.

Just before the war started, I went to the downtown YMCA to

apply for the front desk clerk's position at swing shift hours, ideal for a student. They were raising funds for the YMCA International World Brotherhood Program. Director Woodbury said, "I received a phone call that there's a position, and they wanted me to send a bright university student over. You're the first one I thought of. So go on down there and the job is there. It should be yours as soon as you tell them that I'm sending you."

I was made to wait for an hour beyond the appointment time, during which I had the opportunity to read the bulletin boards full of pictures and idealistic statements about the YMCA brotherhood program in different parts of the world. When at last my interview came, the associate director appeared uneasy and hesitant. I sensed immediately that he had not anticipated a non-white student. He was a former fieldworker for the YMCA in China, so he had foreign experience and an idea of the World Brotherhood Program in a real sense, not just the paper sense of somebody who has never left the United States. He started off by telling me about the World Brotherhood Program. I said, "Yes, I have a pretty good picture of it. I had lots of time to look over your advertisement downstairs." Then he said how difficult it was to raise funds to run programs like that. He came down to saying that this was a businessmen's YMCA downtown, and they wanted a good part of their contributions to come from them. It was not my intent to be discourteous, but I felt a responsibility to let him go through all the discomfort he felt. He finally had to spell it out: "The job is not for you. Nothing personal, you understand. But since the YMCA had to raise money to run these World Brotherhood Programs, it could not risk alienating potential contributors among the businessmen who use the Y."

It was now quite clear to me that the job was out. I said, "I wonder about the inconsistency of violating the spirit of world brotherhood." He turned red and couldn't speak for awhile. After we had been in discussion for about twenty minutes, it was clear to me that my point was made. "Well, I appreciate the time you've given me. I think I understand what the situation is. I think the interview is over." I left.

When I got back, Director Woodbury asked, "How'd it go? When are you starting?" I told him what happened. I'll never forget his face, expressing the pain he was feeling because of his having exposed me to the situation.

I told him, "I appreciate how you're feeling, but it's not the first time this has happened, so it's nothing new to me. I'm not hurting like I think you are. You don't have to worry about what pain you afflicted me with. I grew up with this dichotomy. Learning about the U.S. Constitution—all men, they said all 'men,' not all persons, are created equal—learning all that in civics classes, but daily experiencing restrictions and cut-downs instead of equality. It's nothing new. You don't have to worry about what pain you afflicted me with by having gone down there for an interview. It's just another verification of the society we live in and the work we have to do to overcome those things." That was an experience I never forgot.

Looking back at it, I'm sure that Director Woodbury knew what I was talking about. One of my instructors at the University, Herb King, was African American. Herb took a liking to me because I was writing about prejudice, but from a limited angle, as far as he was concerned. We met that way in 1940. Woodbury had known King back in Texas. Whenever King went to this town in Texas, he would call this friend of his, later a University of Washington executive, and they would work out ways to get together socially. At a certain time in the evening, this friend would sneak King into his house as he couldn't entertain King socially in this bipolar society. Woodbury would join them.

After summer school in 1940, Director Woodbury said, "We are going to send you to the President's Summer School in New York, the training program for the officers of the student Christian movement, the YMCA, and the YWCA." There were twenty-five students, mostly from New England and the southern states, of both genders. I was one of the three from the University of Washington who was sponsored and sent there; the others were Jean, the daughter of a Congregational minister, and Jack Merner, who was a fellow YMCA officer and later a longtime Congregational minister.

We organized our extracurricular activities using free or inexpensive museums and eating places. I found in New York City that the only restriction I had to consider about our chosen program was whether I could afford it or not. It then struck me. In Seattle, I always considered, as second nature, whether I would be turned back at the door for racial reasons. In New York, I didn't have to think about being Japanese, or whether I would be embarrassed or kicked out at the door. That is not to say that New York City didn't have prejudice at that time, as they had pronounced prejudice against Jews and blacks, but there wasn't particular pressure against people of Japanese ancestry. I didn't know that I had that kind of freedom before. In New York, I was experiencing a new dimension of freedom and equality.

The program's organizers developed various kinds of recreational programs using the subway, which cost a nickel at the time. We went to a number of museums that were free and visited places like Father Divine's havens—or "heavens," as some people called them—with chicken dinner for fifteen cents.

On my return trip from New York, one Oregon State guy and I hitchhiked to half a dozen places in the South. We got addresses from our southern friends from the summer program. We said we would like to visit their homes and see which place had the best fried chicken. We hitchhiked down to Washington, D.C. Our friend from the program wasn't there, but her mother said, "We were expecting you." She took good care of us and arranged for tours to the government offices, all of which was new to us.

When we got to the Carolinas, we ran into the color line and Jim Crow laws. We took the city bus, and right in front it says: "North Carolina State Law; White persons, six seats up in the front. Colored people, six seats from the back." I knew I wasn't white, but I didn't know if I was colored. Because I opposed this law in principle, I said to Jim, "Let's go sit up in front. There's a seat opposite the bus driver; let's sit up there 'cause we got on in the middle of the bus. Let's challenge this thing." We could have had trouble. The driver could have thrown Jim off, as they considered him colored. Probably both of us could have been thrown off, but nothing happened.

How could I hold the ideal of first-class citizenship as a viable and realistic option, on the one hand, while knowing about the second-class treatment that was the norm for important positions, on the other hand? At the time, there were no civil service jobs available to us. Nor were there professional engineering and public school education positions for us. The Nisei could be in the top ten in terms of whatever, and the best they could do was to work as a clerk or something in their parents' or Japanese-owned businesses.

During that time, some Nisei went to Japan, trying to get a job that was closer to our profession, but they ran into prejudice there, too, because of not being properly mannered or not speaking Japanese well enough. The Nisei were looked down upon in Japan. You might end up teaching English to Japanese on the side, since Japanese are avid students of English. We found it very difficult to get other kinds of jobs. If we moonlighted, Japanese would find us useful because we were bilingual. We knew what their problems with expression were, and we could correct them, and they could explain questions in Japanese so that we could translate them properly in English. But then they would turn around and hire Caucasian-looking people, Germans or Frenchmen whose English pronunciation was actually abominable. You know, until they become acclimated to English, the French and Germans speak with a distinct accent that is sometimes difficult to understand. Most Americans would know right away that it's a foreigner speaking. But the Japanese would favor them over us. That was the norm in the pre–World War II days. Their looking down on us isn't completely over. So the Nisei didn't find either country very attractive, in terms of getting the kind of first-class treatment that someone of Japanese ancestry would expect.

Not getting a job wasn't a big psychological setback to me. It was just another verification that even in terms of the "friendly" institutions, and even with the support of solid recommendations, we had our difficulties. I decided something important, following the realization that first-class citizenship is a viable objective. If I have to give that up, I might have to live with that reality and accept it, but maybe I could also work so that a little bit of change might take place. In either case, I chose this to be a viable reality that I could live for. I may not get it, but I can live for it. Now if I'm going to keep that with some integrity, I've got to say that these are things that are happening but they're going to change. And I'm not going to accept some of those realities—I'm going to try to live like an American, regardless.

RELIGIOUS EDUCATION IN COLLEGE

You could say that at the University of Washington I was doing "religious studies" through my activities in the student YMCA and the student Christian movement. Howard Scott (my roommate) and I visited the different churches in the district, and we would attend University Temple, which was right across the street. We went largely because we liked the organist. The music there was outstanding.

Sometimes we would go to the Unitarian church because we liked their latitude. There was also Reverend Andrews, the minister in a Japanese American Baptist church. The Quakers were supporters of the groups we were involved with, so Howard and I would drop in on the Quakers. We began to realize we had a special affinity for the Society of Friends, and we found ourselves gravitating over there more and more frequently. After a while we weren't shopping around. It turned out that, in many ways, there were similarities between this group and my parents' orientation. We attended their meetings and some of their social activities regularly and got to know many of them through invitations to their homes.

I delved quite a bit into Quaker history and philosophy and came to understand much better the bases for Quaker belief and faith. In the *Friends Journal*, there was an article, "The Quaker Soul."

> The quickening of the seeker's heart leads to enduring peace as he
> obeys God's leadings. The inward Christ roots out that which is
> selfish, impels us to share our brother's suffering and leads us into
> that which brings unity and peaceful relationships. Such a peace has
> been a healing in our Society today. Our hope lies in a new upsurge
> of power in our meetings, in small devotional groups and in wider
> fellowship. No matter how difficult the situation before us, if we are

owned by the active power of the Lord at all times, we find that we belong to the Kingdom of God, and that we really trust the Lord in every situation.

Floyd Schmoe, a Seattle Quaker elder and community service leader, is certainly an unusual person—kind of an unorthodox rebel. He has energy and ideas. He is a former park naturalist at Mount Rainier. He was teaching in the School of Forestry at the University of Washington but had a special setup. He would teach two quarters and then take off on visiting lectureships to Hawaii, Kansas, or Mexico. He bought a yacht and supported it by organizing educational tours. He lectured on the educational tours on his yacht and gave lectures at the Washington Museum. He was one of the originators of the local American Friends Service Committee, which supported and helped the Japanese Americans who were being sent to concentration camps. Later on, after the U.S. entered the war, I dropped out of the University of Washington during the spring term and volunteered with the AFSC to aid the Japanese Americans. I had found another place where I wanted to work. The AFSC turned out to be closer to my interests than even my work for the student YMCA, although their activities could be done very well hand in hand.

While at the President's Summer School during the summer of 1940, I went to seminars with guys like A. J. Muste, Frank Olmstead, Dr. Evan Thomas, Norman Thomas, Bayard Rustin, all members of the War Resisters League for Peace and Freedom, and advocates of social action and opposition to war and war preparation. I guess I was ready for that because I was just eating that up. It all made sense to me.

PART II

Challenges and Incarceration

AFTER THE UNITED STATES ENTERED WORLD WAR II, GORDON followed a variety of local newspapers on a daily basis. He assiduously cut out articles and pasted them in scrapbooks. Most of the articles he collected indicate that all persons of Japanese or part-Japanese ancestry within the Western Defense Command's military zones were going to be subject to informal and formal restrictions at different levels, including curfew and possible removal.

Very quickly after they were announced, Gordon determined that the curfew order and the order to report for incarceration at a Wartime Civil Control Authority detention camp (or "assembly center"), which in this case was a hastily erected facility built at the fair grounds in Puyallup, Washington, were based on discriminatory and thus unconstitutional policies.

Part II details Gordon's decision to resist the curfew order and mass incarceration and the consequences of his stance. He was jailed, first, in King County Jail in Seattle, even as his challenges evolved into court cases. These writings are the most revealing in terms of offering a detailed sense of what was going on in his mind at the time. After getting out of jail on bail while his trial was pending, Gordon decided to make himself useful by aiding Japanese Americans who had resettled in Spokane, Washington, outside the Western Defense Command's military zones. He was able to reunite briefly with the rest of the Hirabayashi family during this period, while he worked for Floyd Schmoe and the American Friends Service Committee.

When the U.S. Supreme Court upheld Gordon's conviction on the charge of violating the curfew order, he had to hitchhike down to Arizona, where he served additional time at the Catalina Federal Honor Camp, a work camp where prisoners labored to build a highway through the mountains. (Ironically, more than fifty-five years after the fact, the Catalina Federal Honor Camp area was renamed the Gordon Hirabayashi Recreation Site by the administrators of the Coronado National Forest.)

In 1944, Gordon was tried and convicted a second time. On this occasion, his trial had to do with his refusal to fill out the government's so-called loyalty questionnaire. He was sentenced to serve at McNeil Island Penitentiary, located in the Puget Sound not far from Tacoma. Gordon did most of his time at Dupont, a working farm that used prison labor, which was about three miles from the main penitentiary buildings.

While imprisoned and during his time in Spokane, Gordon's relationship with Schmoe's daughter, Esther, blossomed into a courtship. They would marry in 1944, although a second conviction for refusing to register for the draft would separate them again when Gordon was sentenced to a year in a federal penitentiary. Gordon would see his first-born twin daughters only when he was released from McNeil Island in 1945. Although Gordon and Esther eventually divorced after decades of being together, there is no doubt that his profound relationship with her, as well as with her father, were cornerstones in his ability to withstand the day-to-day as well as longer-term pressures that he faced as a student in his mid-twenties, jailed for his beliefs.

CHAPTER 4

World War II

RETURNING FROM NEW YORK, I BECAME ONE OF THE LEADERS of the UW student conscientious objectors group right after the first peacetime conscription law [Selective Training and Service Act of 1940] was passed. We were using the YMCA as a meeting place. We needed to discuss many things, with war fever rising. Colonel Kimmel of the University of Washington Reserve Officer Training Corps (ROTC) was also chairman of the YMCA board, and he actually supported my position as a representative of the conscientious objectors.

Howard Scott and I had similar positions regarding the draft. We also discussed with some people about not just freelancing around in terms of attending different churches, so we began to consider the Society of Friends, which led to our application for membership. We became Quakers in November 1941. I felt most comfortable explaining my beliefs to them, and they were the most adaptable and accepting of my position and understood it the fastest.

As for confronting the government, with all the information I had, I thought, "They're wrong!" For me, my position was a positive one, that of desiring to be a conscientious citizen. It was this desire that prevented my participation in the military as a way of achieving peace and democracy and other ideals for which we stood. How could you achieve nonviolence violently and succeed? War never succeeded before. War has always caused more problems than it solved. I can't say it's wrong for everybody, but I can't approve of it for myself. I couldn't put my life on the line and put my efforts toward war with how I feel.

I wanted to work toward justice and peace in my own way. And there were others with whom I could do that, namely, liberal members of churches and political parties. We had a lot of protection actually. If we had to go to prison, treatment was all right, since the concept of conscientious objection was not ipso facto disloyal.

On Sunday, December 7, 1941, I went to the Quaker meeting as usual. After the meeting, a student came down from an apartment across the street: "I skipped the meeting this morning. Japan bombed Pearl Harbor! We're at war!" It didn't sound real. It was unbelievable, but it slowly sank in.

On February 19, 1942, President Franklin D. Roosevelt, acting under his emergency war powers, issued Executive Order 9066, which delegated broad powers to the secretary of war as well as U.S. military commanders to protect the national security. That protection included the right to remove any suspect individuals from military areas.

A proclamation, generally referred to as the curfew order, was issued on March 24, 1942, restricting the movement of certain individuals. General John L. DeWitt, who was the top military man in charge of the Western Defense Command, issued the curfew. It was applied to all enemy aliens—Germans, Italians, Japanese, plus non-aliens of Japanese ancestry—confining them to their residences between 8 p.m. and 6 a.m., and restricting their travel to areas within a radius of five miles from their homes. The government and military kept using this term "non-alien" in identifying the second-generation Japanese Americans, who, after all, were actually U.S. citizens by birthright. The military seemed to feel more comfortable carrying out these orders if they didn't have to think about applying them to other Americans. At first I responded as an ordinary citizen and obeyed government orders.

As I thought the situation over, however, I reasoned that a citizen is a member of a state: a person, native or naturalized, who owes allegiance to a state and is entitled to protection from it. An alien is someone who is not a citizen. What, then, is a "non-alien"? I felt forsaken as a citizen to be included in this strange kind of categorization. It appeared that the federal government was more interested in suspending citizens' rights than in protecting constitutional guarantees regardless of race, creed, or national origins.

At my YMCA dormitory, there were about fifteen of us, mostly locals, but some from different states and a few internationals: one or two Chinese, a Filipino, and some Canadians. They became my timekeepers. "Gordon, it's five to eight," and I would rush back from the library, which was about two blocks from my UW dormitory, Eagleson Hall. And then it happened. One night, I thought to myself, "I can't do that. I have to change my philosophy or I can't do this, or I'm not true to myself, and if I'm not, I'm not a very good citizen to anybody. Why am I dashing back and those guys are still down there, and I could stay longer and get some more work done, too?"

So I went back to the library, and the first dorm mate who saw me said, "Hey! What are you doing here?"

I said, "What are you doing here?"

"Working," he responded.

I retorted, "Well, I've got work to do, too, same as you. Why should I be running back if you're not running back? We're both Americans!"

My dorm mates never turned me in. They could have. I never was arrested for curfew violation or caught as I was roaming around the University District. If I had been living a half a block away at the Japanese Students Club, I would have been one of the forty or so residents who would be returning at five to eight. If that had been the case, I wonder whether openly confronting the racist curfew order would have occurred to me?

If I were to maintain my integrity in terms of my belief that I am a first-class American citizen, but then accepted second-class status, I would have had to accept all kinds of differences. But how is it that I could raise a question about being a first-class citizen when every day I experience differences that restrict my rights because of my ancestry?

The curfew and exclusion orders were issued, making the Nisei subject to those restrictions purely on the grounds of ancestry, but many Nisei found it possible to find a way to accept those orders in the name of loyalty and patriotism. I heard various reports from the Japanese community. Nisei came to have their lunch at the YMCA, and I dropped over to the Japanese Students Club from time to time. I heard that the Issei leaders were being picked up. Among the community, all sorts of rumors were rife, and the concentration camp fever hit us all. Others will be picked up. There was a kind of resignation among us that because the Issei were prohibited from naturalizing, they were still Japanese subjects. And with war, they were technically enemy aliens. Therefore we expected that some restrictions would fall on them, that they would all be put into some kind of confinement. I remember trying to assure the Issei that, at worst, some things like that could happen, but if they did, we Nisei would look after their needs.

Shortly after the curfew order, the government posted an official proclamation on telephone poles and post office bulletin boards: NOTICE TO ALL PERSONS OF JAPANESE ANCESTRY, BOTH ALIEN AND NON-ALIEN. Civilian Exclusion Order No. 57 commanded all Japanese and Japanese Americans out of their homes and into special, totally segregated, camps.

Soon enough, the districts of Seattle were on a deadline to move all persons of Japanese ancestry, "both alien and non-alien." All this time I was thinking that when the last bus came, I would probably be on it. About two weeks before my time came, I said to myself, "If I am defying the curfew, how can I accept this thing? This is much worse, the same principle, but much worse in terms of uprooting and denial of our rights, and the suffering it's going to cause." While I had to agonize over that for a couple of days, the answer was inevitable. I found it necessary to keep myself internally intact.

I was a senior at the University of Washington. At the end of winter term in March 1942, I dropped out of the university. It was clear to me that I would not be around long enough to complete spring session. I volunteered for the fledgling local American Friends Service Committee, with Floyd Schmoe as my boss. When the Seattle Regional Office of the AFSC was organized, Arthur Barnett was its first clerk; and he and his wife, Virginia, remained active with the committee through the merging of the Seattle and Portland regions into what was the Northwest Regional Office.

The top priority was to sensitively respond to needs arising among the Japanese Americans. The Quakers were responding to calls for help. My assignment involved helping those families with little kids whose Issei fathers had been picked up and interned immediately after Pearl Harbor because they were leaders of the community. The mothers were busy closing the houses, arranging for storage, and preparing young children to carry their things on the trek to camp. Gosh! Something seems wrong; helping people to go behind barbed wires and into flimsy shacks. What a mixed-up life this is—the American way. It really horrified me to help these families pack up their belongings, drive them down to the temporary camp at the Western Washington Fairgrounds in Puyallup, and leave them behind barbed wire. Those who saw me waving good-bye expected to see me within a few weeks, a prisoner myself. Then, somewhere in a period of a few days, it occurred to me that if I can't tolerate curfew, how can I go with this camp deal, which is much worse? As long as I had come to this stage, I thought I couldn't do it. It was only about a week before the last evacuee left, but by then, I knew I wouldn't go!

Bill Makino, a Nisei, a couple years behind me, is a very bright honors student. He was on the YMCA freshman cabinet and later on the senior cabinet. When curfew came in, I happened to be taking care of the furnace in the YMCA. "I have a bunk here, so you can stay here during the week and go home during the weekends. Let's investigate this further and think about it," I told him. We attended discussion meetings, and he was finding that interesting.

At one point, I said, "This thing is all wrong. If I go to camp, I am giving tacit approval of what's going on, so I can't comply."

Bill said, "I can't comply either." So we both decided that we couldn't go along with it. It would be an absolute denial of our rights.

Bill said, "I'm going to have to tell my parents."

I told Bill to go easy and explain it to them. It's bound to be a very touchy situation in terms of people who are afraid. "We've been talking about doing this together, and I would like somebody to share with through this experience, helping each other. But your situation is different than mine, and your parents are really asking you a very important question. I think you should really try to do the right thing all the way around, and if you could convince yourself that because of the stance, you would like to go with me to jail. Because of your family situation and this emergency, you may feel that you have to go with your parents because you are obligated to help them as much as you can. If you talk yourself into doing that, you go with them. You come with me only if you can't go with them because other values and principles make it impossible for you to do so, as much as you love your parents. Then you come with me, and we will try to sort it out." So I gave Bill a way to rationalize an alternative position.

That's how we started out together, and maybe two weeks before it came to a crisis, he had to tell his parents and came back looking like somebody died or something. Bill said, "I talked to my parents. They were shocked, and they gave me the works." His parents were counting on him, and they begged him. "We don't know where we're going and what the government's doing, but one thing we could do is try to keep together." He was the only child, and his father was sixty years old. For me, Dad was fifty-two, Ed just finished high school, and Jim is a sophomore, so if I was out of the picture, the family was still in good hands.

As it turned out, at the end of March 1942, just on the eve of my going to the CPS [Civilian Public Service] Camp at Cascade Locks in Oregon, they rescinded my order without any explanation. I found out later it was because they suspended all actions on conscription relative to Japanese ancestry, and all Japanese Americans were reclassified as 4-C, or "aliens ineligible for service." Still, my earlier conscientious objector stand contributed in various ways toward my decision to resist evacuation. My position was a positive one, that of desiring to be a conscientious citizen. It was this desire that, for me, prevented participation in the military as a way of achieving peace and democracy and other ideals for which we stood. Although I had dropped out of the university, I arranged to remain in the YMCA dorms and continue my job of tending the furnace and sweeping the floors.

My parents, who still lived in Thomas, were expecting to be uprooted sometime in May, and because we lived south of Seattle, the family was initially going to be sent to the center for Japanese Americans erected at Pinedale, California. They thought that I would be home in time to join them for the exodus. I had to explain what was happening to me and tell them that I would not be joining them. Because of travel restrictions and demands on my time by the Quaker service work, I had to telephone home to give my parents the unpleasant news.

My mother pleaded, "Please, put your principles aside on this occasion, come home, and move with us. Heaven knows what will happen to you if you confront the government. You are right and I agree with you, but this is war. We're all facing unknowns. We are going to be moved, but we don't know where or for how long. The worst of all would be that if we are separated now, we may never get together again."

That was quite a concern to her if I continued to defy the government. My brother Ed heard Mom crying and begging. She had read *The Count of Monte Cristo*, and as that was her only reference to jails and prisons, she worried about the consequences of my decision. I might face the firing squad or something like that. I told her, "If I change my mind because of your pressure, it wouldn't be good. I need to retain my own self-respect, because when I take this stand, I am following what I think is right. I can't change my views, since I'd rather remain true to my beliefs and be true to you as your son."

After the war, my brother Ed observed, "Once they had done all they could do to dissuade Gordon and saw they couldn't change his mind, they became his greatest supporters and were proud of him, in spite of the terrifying thought of his being in prison."

As for my parents' influence, I think they were always a part of the picture. I carried on from their influence and applied it to areas that they wouldn't have, such as politics. When my mother heard my reasons, she complimented me for straight thinking and having the courage to make such a decision. She agreed with the soundness of my position and said that she and Dad wholeheartedly supported my stand. After I hung up, a considerable time elapsed before the tears on my cheeks and in my heart dried. Because of my strong family ties, I felt guilty for a long time.

When my family was eventually moved from Pinedale to the more permanent War Relocation Authority [WRA] camp known as Tule Lake in Northern California, two women who had been uprooted from the Los Angeles area trudged the dusty road from the opposite end of the camp looking for my mother. When they finally located her, they said they had heard that the mother of the fellow in jail fighting for their rights was housed in that block. They had come to greet her and to say "Thank you!" In recounting this episode, my mother wrote about what a great lift she had received from that visit. When I read her letter, I experienced a sudden removal of weight from my shoulders, which I hadn't realized I was carrying. I knew then that nothing I could have said or done could have given her more satisfaction.

In any case, as I prepared to take my stand in Seattle, I heard about Min [Minoru] Yasui in Portland and his refusal to obey the curfew because his case was already going on. As far as the Japanese American community was concerned, in terms of the norms of the 1940s, protesting was not a frontline activity, not even a backline option. The Japanese American Citizens League (JACL) was the big thing in the Japanese community. I knew the leaders, men like Jimmy Sakamoto and Bill Hosokawa. They were working on opposite things from what I was doing, so I never consulted them.

Had Japanese American leaders known of my position while they were still in Seattle, they would have confronted me and said, "You are not even dry behind the ears. How can you take such a step that will create difficulties for the whole group? How do you know there won't be a backlash? How do you know you are right and the rest of us are wrong?" I would have had difficulty answering their questions. But I would have had questions for them also. How could they defend America and the Constitution by acceding to a decision made by military authorities to suspend constitutional guarantees, especially when there had been no suspension of the Constitution via martial law? In the end, I would not have changed their views, and they would not have changed mine. By personality, though, while I had independent positions on various things, I was never what you might call the kind of person who habitually protested.

As I followed the press after the U.S. entered the war, the writing was on the wall. The first part of the evacuation process began with the Bainbridge Islanders, who, because of their proximity to naval installations, were moved in March 1942. The last district in Seattle to be evacuated was the northeast section, including the University District, where I was living. The deadline was May 12, 1942. By the end of March, the Bainbridge Island Japanese Americans were gone. At that point, I knew that I wasn't going. I sat down and wrote a statement:

WHY I REFUSE TO REGISTER FOR EVACUATION

Over and above any man-made creed or law is the natural law of life—the right of human individuals to live and to creatively express themselves. No man was born with the right to limit that law. Nor, do I believe, can anyone justifiably work himself to such a position.

Down through the ages, we have had various individuals doing their bit to establish more securely these fundamental rights. They have tried to help society see the necessity of understanding those fundamental laws; some have succeeded to the extent of having these natural laws recorded. Many have suffered unnatural deaths as a result of their convictions. Yet, today, because of the efforts of some of these individuals, we have recorded in the laws of our nation certain rights for all men and certain additional rights for citizens. These fundamental moral rights and civil liberties are included in the Bill of Rights, U.S. Constitution, and other legal records. They guarantee that these fundamental rights shall not be denied without due process of law.

The principles or the ideals are the things which give value to a person's life. They are the qualities which give impetus and purpose toward meaningful experiences. The violation of human personality is the violation of the most sacred thing which man owns.

This order for the mass evacuation of all persons of Japanese descent denies them the right to live. It forces thousands of energetic, law-abiding individuals to exist in a miserable psychological and a horrible physical atmosphere. This order limits to almost the full extent the creative expressions of those subjected. It kills the desire for a higher life. Hope for the future is exterminated. Human personalities are poisoned. The very qualities which are essential to a peaceful, creative community are being thrown out and abused. Over 60 percent are American citizens, yet they are denied on a wholesale scale without due process of law the civil liberties which are theirs.

If I were to register and cooperate under those circumstances, I would be giving helpless consent to the denial of practically all of the things which give me incentive to live. I must maintain my Christian principles. I consider it my duty to maintain the democratic standards for which this nation lives. Therefore, I must refuse this order for evacuation.

Let me add, however, that in refusing to register, I am well aware of the excellent qualities of the army and government personnel connected with the prosecution of this exclusion order. They are men of the finest type, and I sincerely appreciate their sympathetic and honest efforts. Nor do I intend to cast any shadow upon the Japanese and the other Nisei who have registered for evacuation. They have faced tragedy admirably. I am objecting to the principle of this order, which denies the rights of human beings, including citizens. [May 13, 1942]

I circulated a half-dozen copies to the chairman of the YMCA board; Colonel Kimmel, director of the University of Washington ROTC; and a few YMCA supporters. Dr. Fred Ring said, "I just heard about your position—that you intend to refuse to go along with this. I admire your position . . . but I'm trying to determine whether this is a courageous act or a foolhardy act." And he was seriously reviewing for himself whether mine was an intelligent way of expressing my objections. Once I was in jail, however, both he and his wife, Mabel, both of whom were Baptist Church and Fellowship of Reconciliation members, were right there supporting me.

CHAPTER 5

Arraignment Summons

AS REMOVAL FROM SEATTLE DREW NEAR, IT OCCURRED TO ME that if I couldn't tolerate curfew, then how could I agree to be evacuated, which is much worse? I had ignored the curfew order, but the exclusion order was different. If I were roaming the streets, sooner or later I'd be accosted and picked up. On May 16, 1942, I made arrangements with Arthur Barnett to meet me in the morning after the last busload of Japanese left, and he'd drive me over to the FBI. We did this and on the duly appointed day met Special Agent Francis Manion. Barnett said, "My name is Arthur Barnett. I'm Gordon's legal advisor, and we feel that it is appropriate for us to come here to present this to you. We're not trying to hide anything or defy the authorities. It's just that this is the way we feel."

Barnett gave him a copy of "Why I Refuse to Register for Evacuation." Agent Manion said, "Oh, we already have that." I was told that I had dropped a copy on the street the day before and a woman picked it up and called the FBI, who sent an agent to pick it up.

I said, "Here is the original; I'd like to leave it with you."

He said, "Okay, we'll take it."

I continued, "I only circulated half a dozen. I'm kind of curious how you got it."

He said, "Well, we might use this source again, so we'd rather not divulge it."

I don't think I dropped it on the street. It was only after thinking about it that I realized it probably was Colonel Kimmel, chairman of the YMCA board and director of the University of Washington ROTC. I think he felt that, since I was violating a wartime proclamation, it was his duty to turn my statement over to the FBI. Today, it seems reasonable to me, and I understand that that's what he was obliged to do. It's a duty thing, so he needed to follow his military line of responsibility.

After conferring with Assistant U.S. Attorney Gerald Shucklin, who advised that I be given a chance to register for evacuation, Agent Manion drove me directly to the Maryknoll Registration Center, one of the Catholic schools used for registration. After a considerable wait, they said, "You're supposed to sign here."

I said, "That looks like the same registration form I saw a few days ago. Has there been any change in it? No? Well, I can't sign it any more than last week."

Manion responded, "If you don't sign, you're violating the law, and you're subject to some punishment."

I retorted, "I can't do it. What you are going to do as a result of my inability to sign, that's for you to determine. I don't make my decisions on the basis of what I think you're going to do."

Manion took me to a military post, Fort Lawton, and gave me another opportunity to sign. I said, "This is the same form, and I can't sign it." Toward the end of the day, they brought me to the King County Jail, Tank 3C.

Captain Michael A. Revisto, adjutant of the Wartime Civil Control Administration in Seattle, came to see me in jail. There were three headquarters on the West Coast in charge of the uprooting of the Japanese. Revisto, ironically, was an Italian American whose alien relatives were also "enemy aliens." He was cordial and wanted me to register. He reminded me of the violations charged against me: being in an excluded area, refusing to register with the authorities, not being in camp. "The Western Defense is ready to drop everything. We'll give you private escort to Puyallup." I learned that Seattle was the only one of the three western headquarters that didn't have a "perfect record."

Trying to be cooperative: "I can't do that. Get some guy to carry me to the car, drive over there, and dump me inside the camp gate."

Revisto: "I can't do that."

I was flabbergasted. "You mean, you could help process all of the Japanese Americans without any charge except on the grounds of ancestry, and in clear conscience, you can't do this?" Whenever possible, I tried to separate the objectionable issue from the person administering it. I succeeded in making some good friends that way, and it made it easier to maintain my objections to the issue.

Isn't it interesting how one little incident can stop a person so completely? FBI agent Manion had confiscated my briefcase and found my diary. I had begun my diary the first of May, anticipating some new and strange experiences. During the initial discussion, we had this exchange: "You know, there was another restriction you faced. What did you do about that?"

I responded, "What's that?"

He said, "The curfew restriction. It's in your diary. Were you out after 8 p.m. last night?"

I answered, "Yes. Like you and other Americans, so was I."

Manion: "Oh, then you violated the curfew, too. That would be a 'count two' violation."

I said, "Are you turning yourself in for curfew violation, since you did exactly as I did, and we are both Americans?"

Manion: "Ah, but you are of Japanese ancestry."

I argued, "Has the U.S. Constitution been suspended?"

Manion: "No, not to my knowledge."

I added, "Then, how could a general issue an order that violates the Constitution and the rights of citizens regardless of race, religion, national origin, or creed?"

Manion: "You'll have to take that up with the judge!" We both smiled a little.

In his report to the FBI on our initial discussion, Agent Manion wrote: "It is the principle of the Society of Friends that each person should follow the will of God according to his own convictions. . . . He [Gordon Hirabayashi] could not reconcile the will of God, a part of which was expressed in the Bill of Rights and the U.S. Constitution, with the order discriminating against Japanese aliens and American citizens of Japanese ancestry."

On May 20, I appeared before U.S. Commissioner Harry Westfall for a preliminary hearing: "Subject admitted his failure to comply with the exclusion order and was bound over to the grand jury under bond of $5,000." The bail was conditioned on the basis of my release and transfer to the Puyallup center, where I had been driving fellow Japanese Americans.

Bail was set, but it wasn't acceptable to me. At first they said $500. I asked, "Does that mean if we put up the $500, I'll be released like anybody else?"

They checked and said two things: "First, the bail is changed to $5,000, and, second, if that is posted, then you will be released to a camp."

It bothered me, as by posting bail under these conditions, I would be agreeing to go to a camp. "I can't accept that. I should be released like anybody else."

The judge declared, "I have to abide by the regulations, which say this area excludes all Japanese."

I turned it down on principle.

On May 24, I refused to sign a five-page statement admitting curfew violations, and Agent Manion turned it over to the U.S. attorney's office. Four days later, after amending the initial complaint, the federal grand jury returned an indictment that charged me with two violations of Public Law 503: the first charge was violation of the exclusion order, and the second charge was for curfew violation.

My lawyer, Frank Walters, submitted a plea for abatement, stating that I was a native-born citizen of good standing and as such should receive the benefits thereof. Therefore, I should not be incarcerated any longer but should be released immediately. The hearing for this plea was scheduled for June 13. It was very doubtful that the judge would do other than refuse to accept it. Inasmuch as citizenship was being completely ignored, I felt this plea was a wise legal move.

THE DEFENSE COMMITTEE

Washington state senator Mary Farquharson, whose husband was a professor at UW and on the board of the YMCA, had heard about my arrest and was looking all over for me. It wasn't until her staff made all sorts of phone calls that they finally tracked me down in the federal tank of the King County Jail, where I was to remain for the next nine months. She visited me. "I heard this rumor and wanted to check it out. I just talked to someone, and I was told you decided to buck this order."

I said, "That's right. I don't see how I could conform to it and still be the person I want to be. I have to change my philosophy and my beliefs about the American Constitution to go ahead with this, and I don't want to do that. I want to keep my beliefs, so I've got to buck this."

She said, "Tell me about it . . . I support you 100 percent. Many of us just feel this is such a tragic event. We are upset that our civil liberties are being eroded. We protest it, but it's very difficult to find a way in which we could make our protest effective. We wanted to know whether you're going to be carrying on a test case or not."

I said, "At the moment I just took a stand, and I'm not thinking about a test case because I am not informed about the legal ramifications. I certainly do not have the financial resources."

And then she said, "Because of these concerns by me and some of my friends, we wondered, if you're not going to do it, if we could organize a committee to make a test case of it. Not only would we make a test case of it; we're going to use this case as a foundation to request speaking engagements whenever there's a forum or something or church conference. This needs to be protested!"

Gordon Hirabayashi Defense Committee! That's how the letter-head on the stationery read. Boy, it was certainly official-sounding. It sounds kind of funny, too, especially when they spell my whole name out. People will stumble over that last name, but I imagine that if people ever learn it once, they won't easily forget it. The committee members were people I knew and respected: Ray Roberts, chairman; Mary Farquharson, secretary-treasurer; Arthur Barnett; J. E. McRae; Anna T. Milburn; Mrs. Harry M. Myers; Arthur Redman; Amy Smith; and the Reverends U. G. Murphy, James Brett Kenna, and Allan Lorimer. The committee included professors, businesspeople, ministers, civil liberties advocates, Quakers, and members of peace organizations.

Besides being a Washington state senator, Mary Farquharson is a YWCA advisor, member of the Church of the People and the FOR [Fellowship of Reconciliation], and active in the Student Christian Movement. She used to come to our retreats and so forth as a resource person and spoke on issues related to women's causes, minorities, and so on. She became my chief motivator. Arthur Barnett, my personal legal advisor, is a Quaker and a member of FOR. His wife, Virginia Barnett, is quite active in the YWCA and an executive of the National American Friends Service Committee. Ray Roberts, an ordained minister, is a businessman in the community, on the YMCA board, and a former YMCA director in China. Other supportive people include Reverend Fred Shorter, Church of the People; Ev McRae, manager of the University Book Store; Floyd Schmoe, Quaker and field secretary of the Seattle American Friends Service Committee; and M. D. Woodbury, director of the YMCA. Were it not for this wartime group in Seattle who braved catcalls of treason, disloyalty, and "enemy lover" to battle for citizen rights, my case would probably have remained an obscure lower court decision.

The plan was to form a local team, with the national American Civil Liberties Union (ACLU) becoming the major sponsor. That had to be changed when Roger Baldwin, the chairman of the national board, phoned Mary Farquharson to tell her that the board had failed to back him up. Several members of the board were so loyal to Franklin D. Roosevelt that they did not wish to do anything to interfere with the war effort. The national board of the ACLU stated: "We have adopted a policy not to contest the constitutional rights of the president as commander in chief regarding the evacuation orders. The government, in our judgment, has the constitutional right in the present war to establish military zones and to remove persons, either citizens or aliens, from such zones when their presence may endanger national security, even in the absence of a declaration of martial law. Such removals, however, are justified only if directly necessary to the prosecution of the war or the defense of national security."

"Yours is the most mixed-up case I've ever run into," Mary Farquharson greeted me that afternoon. She was very much disappointed—even shocked—by the decision of the ACLU board. However, she showed me several letters that she had received. A letter from Nevin Sayre of the FOR said he was very much interested in my case, particularly because I am a pacifist and an FOR member. If the ACLU pulled out, Sayre was sure the FOR could call on its members, nationally, to carry on.

Norman Thomas, who happened to be one of the directors of the ACLU, displayed an interest in fighting the presidential order of February, starting at the beginning. Of course that would be contrary to the resolution. It seemed that the scholastic circulation of the resolution was creating some surprise for those who had voted it in. So many loopholes!

Fred Korematsu's lawyer Ernest Besig had written a letter regarding the strategy of the Northern California group in fighting some cases on the writ of habeas corpus of a few evacuees. Theirs will be an offensive on the grounds of the Bill of Rights and the removal of Nisei on a purely racial or descent basis. Of course, in my case, the same points will be brought out, but it will be on a slightly different circumstance. I, having refused, am a defendant and must meet the government's attacks. Yet Clarence Darrow's favorite and most powerful weapon was to "prosecute the prosecution."

The committee secured the services of Frank Walters, a Seattle lawyer, as my formal attorney to defend me in the district court. Mary Farquharson thought that the ACLU could step in where there were no conflicts with their resolutions and pull out where there was a conflict. At any rate, it seems as though the legal side is prepared to go the limit.

In spite of the position taken by his board, Roger Baldwin wrote that he was very eager to support the case and that the ACLU was still prepared to meet half of my attorney's fees. It seems that there is a very wide range of views, yet the key people want a lot of action. We shall see.

CHAPTER 6

King County Jail

TANK—THEY USE THAT WORD—3C IS THE FEDERAL TANK, AND it has a capacity of forty persons. It has two levels of five cells, with four bunks on each side. There are twenty men over here on this aisle, back-to-back. They all face out. At 6 or 6:30 a.m., they open up and keep the hallways open. Then you go into the day tank, with a table and a metal bench screwed down to the cement right in the center so that forty people can sit down there. It has bars on all sides and hallways on the outside of the bars. We are there half of the day, and the other half we're in the cells. So during the day, people would be playing cards, reading, writing. We don't get any fresh air, and there's no exercise yard. This is a jail; it isn't prison. It's a holding place. So people are here for a few days. For those already sentenced, they're here 'til they're transported to McNeil Island or wherever. Or they're thrown in here, charged with a federal violation of something, and therefore they're waiting until trial. If they can't set bail, they're in here until trial time. So some of them may be in for a month or six weeks, but most of them are here for a shorter time.

I maintained mutually respectful and friendly contacts with most of the prison officials. On the other hand, I felt free to object to things I couldn't accept. I learned early in prison that if I took a stand, there would be consequences. One of the "screws" called Barney is really a mean hombre. Oftentimes he's drunk, or just getting over it, and treats the boys horribly. His language is unnecessarily crude, his tone unnecessarily rasping, his mannerisms unnecessarily impudent. He looks down on us as unwanted criminals. Everyone dislikes him. Last Friday, Barney blew his top. He made all of us in Tank 3C move over to 4C on the grounds that 3C was too crummy. 4C turned out to be infinitely more crummy and dirty. The smell in the cells and on the mattresses was terrific. The boys were getting to the volcanic stage. Protests were made over Barney's head. We are due to move back to 3C. The crew that comes on at 3 p.m., Captain Jarrett et al., are superb. We all wish the morning crew were like them.

Saturday was a unique day. All of us were called out and individually frisked. Then we were jammed into the visitors' compartment while the guards "shook down" the cells and the day tank. I lost a coat hanger and a flattened knife substitute I used as a spreader. When I was being frisked, they missed my pocket watch and they overlooked the inside pocket in my coat so I still have the contents of that pocket. Our thermos bottle was strangely left behind. Gee, it was just a routine shakedown, customary for a new administration to do as they take over, but it was an interesting experience for me. They certainly left the place in a mess! Just like the aftermath of a tornado or a bunch of thieves . . .

We eat twice a day. In the morning, our meal is brought up in beautiful buckets; I used to use similar ones for mops. Mush—rolled oats, cracked wheat, or cornmeal—is the main filler. In another bucket comes milk. It is really amazing the skill with which they have skimmed it. Delicious apricots come in the third bucket, delicious unless you must have some sugar in the sauce. A large square bread container holds four slices for each person. Two medium spoonfuls of sugar come in a bag for each guest. A breakfast is not complete without a good cup of coffee, and therefore we are given a large pot full of brown, saltpetered water.

Our next and last meal for the day comes at 3:30 p.m. The menu varies during the week. On Sunday, it's boiled meat; Monday, stew; Tuesday, beans; Wednesday, meatballs; Thursday, beans; Friday, fish; Saturday, stew. Along with the main entree come boiled spuds, bread, and tea. With boiled meat come gravy and applesauce, very watery. With stew, we get either rice or macaroni. With beans (somehow there's a lot left over), we have coleslaw, commonly referred to as "grass." For meatballs, the match is white beans, and fish comes with peas. Of course from time to time there is a call for salts or CCC pills, anything to promote the call of nature. Sometimes I wonder how we can all survive after a constant diet of that sort. One can easily learn to overlook the dark and dreary buckets that contain this foodstuff, but we can never overcome the urge for green vegetables, and a meal that is not predominantly starchy.

When I first came to this place, I used to wash my dishes industriously after each meal before I would use them again at the next meal. I was so careful and particular about the dust and filth in here. Now, though I still wash industriously after each meal, I only wipe my plates before meals. While I used to wrap up my bread in newspaper or in wax paper (when available), I now merely drop the bread slices in a paper bag. While I used to throw away my food if I discovered a dead cockroach in it or saw a live one crawling on it, I now merely remove the thing and nonchalantly continue my dinner.

Yes, I have changed a bit, and I'm afraid it is not all for the better. But I still maintain some of my standards, such as regular showers at least twice a week, and I always disinfect the shower room. I always use my own cell's toilet even though I see to it that the main tank's toilet is disinfected thoroughly twice a day. I have not yet become accustomed to profanity as an expression of speech, even in my awkward, uncomfortable moments. I keep my hankies, shirts, and socks rotating in regular turns.

Twice a week we shave—Sundays and Wednesdays. As today is Sunday, the boys are all shaving. Nothing ever happens on Sundays except the two visitations by church groups. Yet the men all shave neatly, wash up, comb their hair, and wear their cleanest clothes. I'm beginning to think that, despite their verbal expressions of dislike for the churches and their visitations, inwardly they look forward to it. We are funny creatures. That's what makes us interesting, I guess. That's why there remains hope for us.

Perched on a garbage can turned over, I courageously allowed Ted Takahashi to clip away at my hair. We, the incarcerated, do not have much choice. Ted amateurishly whacked away, no less than four kibitzers took a hand, literally, but according to public opinion, it's not a bad job at all. Forty-five minutes is a long time to sit for just a haircut, though. P.S.: Ted beams with pride every time he looks at me.

I've been up every day since May when I first walked in here. Last Sunday, I found myself ailing and remained in bed. For the first time, I remained in my cell all day. I didn't see the church service but heard it. It was nice and quiet, and very enjoyable. But did the bed get hard! By nightfall, I was so stiff and sore in my back. I had to get up and actually stretch and bend and loosen my arch. These springs aren't too flexible. My throat was sore and I had a headache. Kenji Iki claims I was pale as a corpse; but shucks, that's no symptom any more.

Last weekend, my stomach kicked back on me. I was feeling terrible. The cells being as close and open-air as they are, the fellows could distinctly hear the results of my revolting stomach. The next morning, no less than six persons came around in all sincerity to ask how I was feeling, and if there was anything they could do for me. It was very touching. Who would have expected "jailbirds" to be sympathetic and concerned about something not directly connected with them? Then I realized that they are humans, men with that of God in them, just as I hope I have. God is good. God is love. Whenever there is that expression of kindness, concern, love, and selflessness, we have that much more evidence—that much more experience—that there is a God, an infinite power.

We have almost every kind [of prisoner] represented here. And they, with a couple of barbers, Olympic Peninsula liquor violators, etc., sure twist up the English language. I've been around a lot of athletes when they were sore, but I have never yet heard as much cussing as I have here the past week. And the unique thing of it all is that the cussing comes so naturally and easily that it is beautiful in its own quaint way. It is almost musical, symphonic. I know for a fact that if those cuss words were omitted, the conversation would certainly turn staid, dull, and superficial. Life here is pretty gay. Fellows try hard to avoid gloom and depression and succeed pretty well. Yet most everybody realizes it is but a shell. Personal conversation soon reveals that. Some of the fellows have had previous jail experiences and sort of become callous about it. Others feel they are here because of some raw deal and consider such raw deals the natural thing to expect in life. They shrug it off.

Four dollars were sent in, and I accepted it as the tank banker. In an attempt to democratically decide what to buy, I ran into a stone wall. We are too disorganized, too transient, too unprepared, to practice democracy in the YMCA cabinet style to which I was accustomed. After a consultation of some ten persons, who formed a sort of informal committee, we decided that the best way to use the money was to split it individually; the only stipulation being that they buy food up to the fifteen-cent limit.

They came to regard me as their leading nominee to become their new representative to the jail officials, handling their requests and grievances. They insisted that I become their next mayor.

I retorted, "I don't agree with the way you're running these things. You get somebody else."

They said, "Everybody thinks you're the best, and we don't have any alternate candidate."

They were really putting pressure on me, so I proposed, "Look, if you think I should try, I'll take the position for a week. At the end of the week, we'll assess whether I should continue or not. I will do it my way, and a lot of you may not like it 'cause I believe in nonviolence and in negotiating for things. I don't want to follow the tactics of the kangaroo court that have been used in the past."

They said, "Well, that's fine. You do your own thing, and we will support it."

We had a period of fairly good negotiations with the jail administration regarding some of our grievances and so on. I believe a seed has been planted. I shall attempt to do my part of the cultivation.

According to rumors, we prisoners are charged seventy-five cents to a dollar fifty for room and board. I don't know what the room costs, but our two meals surely do not exceed twenty cents at the most. Perhaps fifteen cents would be the nearer estimate. Although we should all be thankful for what we get and be content, there seems to be a limit beyond which we can ask for human decency. Particularly when it is supposed to be given to us. Somebody is making a good profit somewhere. I will get really curious one of these days and discover for myself who the smart man is.

A week ago, one filthy-looking fellow inmate refused to cooperate. He needed a bath and a shave—immediately. The tank sheriff approached him and was told to go far away from heaven. As this was the accumulation of a week of ornery conduct on the inmate's part, the sheriff and a few others were all for throwing him in the hole or ganging up on on him, shaving him, and throwing him in the cold shower. I wanted one try before I turned the power over to the sheriff. Slowly, guardedly, I approached the man. Casually, I grinned and asked him if he were going to shave.

He stood rubbing his chin and looking down. "Why?"

"Looks to me like you need one. Might make you feel better."

A pause—and then without a word, he walked away.

The next time he walked by me, I asked if he wanted a razor blade. He stopped suddenly and said, "Yeah."

That led to the shave. Now that he had shaved, he sorta wanted a haircut. As Sunday was the occasion for two separate visits by two different church groups, I shared that fact and suggested he take a bath today so his hair will be dry for the clippers tomorrow—all said and done, spick-and-span!

The tank members were amazed. They couldn't figure it out. I had it doped this way: He had developed a negative, chip-on-the-shoulder, suspicious complex. He was unhappy and wanted to be cooperative but was unable to step in gingerly. All he wanted was an opportunity and a way. Remove the occasion for antagonism, and he was your man! The pacifist way is not so helpless, by gar.

Last Sunday afternoon, four evangelists came in for the usual "sing like hell, talk like hell" services. Only this time, it was slightly different. These four (two middle-aged couples) were rather mild in their approach and very likable. The speaker began: "We really came up here to talk to you because we are really interested in you. To prove that we mean it, we're going to send up a basket of something to eat tomorrow. All we want in return is your undivided attention, and to listen to the word of God." I must admit it had favorable results. The inmates listened, or seemed to. The reaction was favorable. No less than eight or nine persons walked up to the bars and spoke to the evangelists and shook hands with them. "They're okay" was the consensus. I could not help but feel that the evangelists' approach was too near bribery. We are confined here; if they have something significant to tell us, we will listen regardless. And if they are sincere, as they were, they should have sent in their presents unannounced the next day, with a little tag attached to it if necessary. They should approach the Samaritan way—Christlike.

About twice a month, two old ladies round out their lives saving the souls of us poor jailbirds. They were in last week. After the service (street-corner type), one of the ladies called me. I was trapped; I had to go. She mentioned that she's seen me for several months. Then she wanted to know if I were saved. As I hesitated a moment, she asked if I had accepted Jesus as my savior. Doggone, Bobby, I was getting sort of fed up about the way they conducted meetings, and it irked me the way she asked me, so I told her I was a Christian and believed as a Christian, although I wouldn't express myself as they did. She said that if you were saved, that was all that mattered—but you've got to be saved. Then she wanted to know if I believed in Jesus. I told her that Jesus's life and teachings were the guiding light in my life. "He is one of my greatest inspirations." That didn't satisfy her. She gave me a brief history of Jesus's life. I thought it too limited and superhuman, so I disagreed.

"Jesus is the Son of God, but so are we."

"Oh, no! That's heresy! He was born of the Virgin Mary and so is not contaminated with the evils of man."

"No, his birth isn't the important thing. It's the way he lived that made him the personality he is."

One thing led to another. Her mouth continually popped open. "Are you saying that Jesus was a bastard? Do you mean to say he did not rise again after his death?"

I quit. She kept emphasizing the importance of the spirit, yet when

I interpret Jesus's life in the spirit of the thing, she wants to hang on to the literal interpretation of the physical part, too. In my opinion, the physical is optional, or, rather, secondary.

It is too late to say these things to two old ladies. It only causes them to pray every night for a Jap boy in jail who is possessed by the devil.

There are many things people don't realize until they meet with predicaments. In jail, you meet those who are paying for being stupid about one thing or another. Also, you really learn it while you're young and less liable to implicate others dependent on you. Besides, it's an eye-opener about how lousy and dirty politics are—boy, I can shock you with some of the facts I've learned. Ninety days in jail will knock out all the cockiness, in addition to giving one a thorough education in the school of the less fortunate.

A big six-foot three-inch Negro and a battling Indian mixed it up for a wild, free-for-all, nothing-barred fight just before our 3:30 meal. The Indian got the worst of it, as buckets, mop wringers, shoes, fists, and the like were used as weapons. As near as I could figure it out, the Negro was writing letters in the seat generally occupied by this Indian. The Indian told him to move since it was time to eat. The Negro told him to wait awhile. Bang! The Indian swung. Then bang, whoosh, crash, jingle jangle, as tin plates and cups scattered off of the tables. It was the wildest, dirtiest fight I ever saw. I hope I don't see another like that. It was too dirty for even a fight enthusiast to enjoy, let alone a fellow with pacifist views. Both boys were separated after awhile by the others in here, as much to protect the Indian's scalp as to end the fight. The superintendent and three deputies were on hand to escort the combatants out. They were sent to the black hole.

Reflecting a bit upon the situation, one wonders why there are not more fights. It is amazing when circumstances are viewed and reviewed. Here we are—approximately forty men in a small low-ceil-inged tank twenty feet by forty feet. There's no room for exercise, the air is foul, the lights are poor, and the noise deafening. A stay of a month or more in this place drives most men to a high nervous pitch. They become irritable and temperamental. Man is not made for close confinement; man must have freedom. He breaks down unless he can maintain his sense of freedom. Most of these boys regard freedom in the physical sense. They seek release, hence the loud noise and occasional fisticuffs.

I have been weighed down with the "executive" responsibilities here. But being a lazy guy, I've split the load three ways among the two most dependable fellows (and likely to stay the longest here) and myself. The three-man council functions smoothly, so far (two whole days). It gave me a chance to step in with alternatives. They could see, even if they aren't converted, that there's always some alternative to violence. And I think the jail management was very pleased. As to that part, they would probably employ some things in similar situations as an alternative, which they might not have before. I think most people who go through an experience of practicing nonviolence feel there's merit to it, though to some extent it depends on you or how you are able to carry it out.

As long as I have been here, and as disgusted as I am with the evils of our present penal system, I cannot get interested in penal reform as a life project. It will certainly be one of my interests, and I shall do all in my power to bring about improvements; but as a life career, I'm more interested in the establishment of personal and social harmony. There is a definite negative correlation between the number of parks and the number of juvenile delinquents in nearly every city. I'm more interested at the moment in ways toward personal and social improvement so that there shall be less need for prisons. Prisons are, in reality, evidence of the weakness and inefficiency of the social system and of the personal deterioration of those in our society. I still believe in the old adage "An ounce of prevention is worth a pound of cure." This is true in most cases, I believe.

Consciously or unconsciously, I've been combating or rather trying to overcome race prejudice and other barriers to a harmonious life most of my life. Yet at this time I'm confronted with a delicate situation. Our tank has about ten Negroes, almost one-third of the total number. About six of them are the noisiest, crudest, dirtiest, "crookedest" group of fellows most of us have ever met. They don't even have honor among themselves. They are incurring the resentment of the others in here. Most of them disgustingly remark, "Dem lousy shinies, I wish they'd put them niggers in another tank." It is too bad that things like this have to happen. I know that the situation is not so because they are Negroes. We have had colored fellows here who were considered among the best fellows we've met. These loud boys happen to be the riffraff, the "Jackson Street Boys." It is the case of an environmental product. The Nisei who are found loitering around Jackson Street are referred to as the "J Street Boys" and are identical in conduct to these colored fellows. Lewd sex talk, even at mealtimes, petty thievery even among their comrades, crude language, loud talk all day long, disregard and disrespect for others quartered here—these things are typical of any group who majors in Jackson Street p.m. activities.

These colored fellows, like the Nisei, want to exert their equality. The only way they know of overcoming their inferiority complex is to outtalk, out-chisel the others. They resent requests for cooperation, feeling each request is an order, as from a person endeavoring to assert superiority. One needs constantly to challenge talk like "All niggers are like that"; at the same time, one needs to challenge the misconceptions harbored by these colored boys. Both are dangerous, as they are outgrowths of certain undesirable attitudes.

With the coming of the primary election, I registered and became a voting citizen for the first time. No one else in our tank voted. It is hard to vote intelligently when you are not very well acquainted with the candidates and the names tell very little. Some sort of previous record ought to be listed in some fair way to help the voters. I suppose that is being done in terms of the campaigns; I don't know. Outside of newspapers, I didn't hear a thing.

There are times when I am perfectly content to lie in my springy bunk and peer through the bars into the dimly lit hallway. I've spent many a night musing, meditating, dreaming, reminiscing, very calm and at peace. But, on the other hand, there are times when I wanted to rip the bars apart and step out, out into the "free world," and look around and reach, reach into the air and gulp it in. I want to see and see. I want to hear good music, good discussion, girls' voices. I want to have a good quiet period. I want and want and want. But they are feelings that come very seldom. That is, I have those feelings often but they are seldom overpowering. Most times, I can maintain some balance. I think that a lot of the inner peace comes from knowing ones like you and your folks, who make Him a clearer, more vivid reality for me.

CHAPTER 7

King County Jail Mates

AS FOR MY FELLOW PRISONERS, IN ROUND FIGURES I WOULD say that maybe 50 percent were there as a result of some kind of wartime regulation violation of one type or another: some resisted the draft or some other type of war-related thing. In other words, they were not your typical "criminal." The others were petty thieves, this and that, in for some sort of criminal violation.

Holy smokes! Six fellows came in yesterday, and we're full up to the brim. Thirty-nine guests, and forty is the capacity. However, several are expected to leave soon, with some bound for the army and others for the road camp at Dupont.

We have a father-son combination in our tank. According to evidence, the father conspired to have his son evade registration for the draft so he might remain at home to support the elderly parents. From what I have been able to gather, the father is definitely guilty. The son, twenty-five years of age, is as pure, innocent, and naive as they come. Here in jail, the father constantly worries about his own release, his own condition. He never even washes his own setups; the KP duties were shoved onto his son.

At the recent trial, the father, who pleaded guilty, was sentenced to fifteen months at McNeil Island Federal Penitentiary. The boy will be inducted into the army. The height of disgust occurred when the father began worrying about who would get the son's pension money and insurance if he is shot, and the father is very concerned that he may not get it. The son, unconscious of all this, does his father's bidding like a trained slave. This morning, the father was called to be taken to McNeil. When the son shook hands with his father, a little emotion could be detected. In spite of everything, he loved his dad; he was emotionally upset and feeling very lonely. For a while, I could not trust myself to approach him. I am glad the son is going into the army, as strict and limited as a soldier's life is. It will mean a new sense of freedom and a view into a new and wider horizon. I wish him well.

One of the more interesting fellows here is a Jehovah's Witness. Currently, he is in Selective Service class 1-A-O, but as an ordained minister, he is requesting class 4-D. Both his local board and the board of appeals have turned down his request, ignoring the affidavits he presented showing his status as a minister. When the induction period came, he landed in jail. His trial comes up on the 14th; he has prepared a remarkable statement of his convictions. His mastery of the Scriptures, their location, etc., is amazing. He has about sixteen quotations and references in his ten-minute appeal. Previously he had twenty. The weakness of his talk was the too numerous quotations, rather than stating things in his own words. The prosecution can scrape up an equal number of quotations to support the military. Also, there was an air of dogmatism—"I have the way"—which may antagonize some of the jurors. To those comments he added a beautiful conclusion, which stated that he was not interested in converting, that he realizes others have other ways of interpreting the Scriptures and he respects their point of view. He respects any person acting upon the dictates of his conscience. These words may not sound natural for a "typical" Jehovah's Witness, but knowing him, I believe him to be entirely sincere. For proof, here I am, a Quaker—quite liberal, definitely not a fundamentalist—and we are good friends. From past records of the court, I fear he will receive a sentence of from three to five years. It is definitely unjust, but he seems prepared to face the consequences.

A pleasant surprise! Our Jehovah's Witness faced the judge for a sentence yesterday. Preceding the sentence, however, the judge was shown the Witness's affidavits as an ordained minister, his honorable discharge from the army, and a short statement of his convictions. He was given eleven months in the road camp, which is the lightest sentence given to a Jehovah's Witness for refusing to be inducted thus far in the nation. We here in the tank were extremely happy because he's such a swell kid and feel that he should be given privileges accorded to other sects' ministers.

A new inmate came into our cell. He is charged on a narcotics violation and is appealing it. At thirty-nine years of age, he has lived a most unique and exciting life. Being of Negro descent with a little Indian thrown in, he's had to battle against societal prejudices. Not content with the usual expected status of a Negro—a porter, a bootblack, etc., and not allowed by the white population to work himself up under ordinary conditions—he learned how to be alert, how to be shrewd, how to outwit the other person. He made it his business to learn all the legitimate ways of stealing. To stay just inside of legitimacy was his aim. During his life, he was never allowed to rise above being a "Negro" except through one means: money. With money, he won respect and prestige. With wealth, he was allowed privileges beyond his expectations. Through this means, he won the reputation, a sincere one, of "He's okay." This reputation will stick even if he becomes penniless. And yet, it isn't money itself that gave him the privileges. It was the power that money represented. I could not deny that money represented power. Yet just how much power does money have? Then it was revealed that a certain amount of money was desirable and essential in the world today, but it is to no avail if it is not accompanied by intelligence. Money, then, he agreed, was a means to an end and should not be used beyond its value.

This new cell mate of ours maintained, "If you have your health, and a little up in the noggin, no one needs to worry about you." I learned all about rackets, white slavery, prohibition, narcotics, lottery, unions, and so forth. Even many churches and sects were cited as rackets. A very prominent Seattle minister, now deceased, was mentioned as the underhand backer of a prostitution ring. I wondered, "Isn't there anything good? Can't honesty prevail?" More power to those who can maintain their principles. Experience teaches most people to have principles but to know how to bend with the wind.

Is betraying your principles merely bending with the wind? I certainly have a lot to learn about the ways of life and about principles in application. I must study and discover what is intelligence, what is stubbornness, what is hypocrisy, what is a compromise, what is maintaining a principle. Many underworld characters have their own code and principles. In their own way, they are honest and reliable. I have added a new friend to my circle.

Two days ago, we welcomed into our fellowship a young fellow, a Eurasian, eighteen years old. For a person of his age, he is remarkably well-read and well-versed on various thoughts concerning life. His father is Japanese, mother is Caucasian. When all but his mother were evacuated last May, he was working in California. When he discovered that he should also be evacuated, he made up his mind to refuse. On Tuesday, he was picked up by the FBI and urged to go on to camp at Puyallup. In that case, they would drop all charges. He refused and was given an attorney, Bruce Bartley. Today, he left on a $100 bond to evacuation quarters until his trial on October 6. His attorney feels they can win the case handily. If that is true, it will be a boon for all concerned, even though he is a Eurasian and not entirely of Japanese descent. His two brothers and sister have been released recently under the rule that people of mixed blood and mixed marriages may leave camp. His father, mother, and younger brothers and sisters are at the War Relocation Authority camp in Idaho.

Another new face in jail is a Japanese alien. Until last May, he was stationed at the lumber mill at National; then on to Puyallup last May; then to Idaho [probably the Minidoka WRA camp, located outside Twin Falls]. After about ten days there, he was suddenly brought here by the U.S. marshal. As yet we do not know exactly why he was brought to King County Jail. The only thing we can figure out is that perhaps he will be deported on the next exchange ship. Under the circumstances, I hope that is true. He has no future here; he will be much happier over there.

There are three Nisei who were involved in the import-export business, and they were accused of selling scrap iron to Japan. One of them was convicted and served a sentence. The two independent import-export people beat their case. There were a few others with some technical draft violations who were in for awhile, but they were sent to camp. It is of interest to note that the original bail for one of these men was set at $50,000. He was acquitted later. Ted Takahashi's bail was $50,000. Kenji Iki's bail was $50,000 but was lowered to $10,000, and he is now in a WCCA camp, called "Camp Harmony," at Puyallup. On the other hand, German espionage suspects like Laura Ingalls and others were bailed at $7,500 and $5,000. Strange things occur during periods of hysteria.

Last night, through Ted Takahashi's interest in business, we got to talking of the immense possibilities in North China following the war. The mineral product is rich in that area, and it has heretofore been undeveloped. With transportation facilities, such as railroads and machinery, the area is open to development. Ted is very much interested in developing that area. He has in mind buying several war industry machineries that will be discarded after the duration and then shipping the whole works for use in China. As a sideline to the conversation, Ted was trying to interest me in either mechanical or electrical engineering. He wants to have two sharp, dependable persons, trained engineers, who will act as his counsel. He'd be willing to send them through school if necessary.

As long as that area has to be developed, it ought to be developed with the least amount of exploitation by someone with social vision. The challenge is so great that I'm almost tempted to go into some engineering field. In fact, I know I would, if I had any interest or abilities along that line. But alas, I'm dumb as an engineer. However, another thought occurred that kept me awake most of last night. If there is such a possibility in North China, there will be another boom, another "westward ho" movement. There will be an influx of all sorts of opportunity-seeking people. The mechanical and material development will swing along in expected fashion, but what is to prevent the lag between material development and social development? Machinery and modern facilities should be a benefit to mankind; but if they go too fast, they have a tendency to enslave mankind.

When people move into new areas, particularly undeveloped, pioneering areas, there will be a painful period of adjustment. Following that will come a period of neglect caused by the need for constant labor in the industries. The social, educational, and religious aspect of individual lives will be well nigh completely ignored. The results will be catastrophic, but the busy people will not realize that. What a place for energetic social engineers to find themselves. What immense possibilities for development of the basic, human side of life. Provincial China will no longer be shut off. With adequate social, educational, religious planning to go along with the material development program, the disasters of so many American "growin' pains" shall be avoided. For a while as I lay there, I forgot completely that I was behind bars. I forgot we were engaged in a messy war. I forgot that following this war there would be a terrible period of depression, of possible diseases, both physical and mental. I forgot everything but the picture of another pioneering community waiting to be developed. It is there either for exploitation by some shortsighted capitalists, or it can be developed with vision and quality.

Ted worked hard to get out on bail. At the moment, there is a fair chance that the bail may be reduced to $5,000, quite a cut from the original $50,000 bail. This was extremely interesting to me, inasmuch as the Eighth Amendment states: "Excessive bail shall not be required, nor excessive fines imposed, nor cruel and unusual punishments inflicted." Ted finally got his bond raised, and left for the WCCA camp at Puyallup. After almost eight months in jail, he had a good-size sea bag full of paraphernalia, including magazines, clothes, medicine, and boxes of this and that. Even at that, he left over half of his things, things we need here but can't get, except through Ted's "ways."

I owe a lot to Ted. He gave me a very essential education on the business side of life and some of the worldly experiences he's had. There are many things on which we disagree, but essentially we both sought the same things in life: happiness and satisfaction that we have lived a full life. His major interest was business, and he played it like a game. He is very honest and straightforward, which are unusual traits for businessmen.

Friday morning, I was busy writing letters. I heard the door clang open and a shout, "Fish!" That told me that a new inmate had just walked in. As I finished the sentence I was writing, I looked up and, lo and behold, there coming toward me was the familiar, golden-brown, expectant face of Kenji Iki! What a pleasant surprise! We shook hands eagerly, and as soon as we got his things in order, we were having a good man-to-man talk. Since we parted company last June, he had gone on to join his family at Puyallup and much had happened . . .

A week ago, Kenji was sentenced to nine years and fined $50,000. Everyone was surprised! It was the first time that Judge Bowen had served such a severe sentence. Many felt that either Bowen has a super-patriotic streak or else he had orders from Washington. In either case, there was evidence that anti-Japanese feeling was gaining momentum even as the Japanese Americans were removed from the West Coast. What hurt Kenji the most was being called disloyal. In his mind, it was merely a business deal—wrong, of course, he realizes that. But there were absolutely no thoughts of disloyalty or of aiding the Japanese. We all hope that following the war, he will be pardoned or his sentence suspended.

Kenji was taking it quite well; he is determined to accept it philo-sophically. Only when he thinks of his wife and the two little ones (four- and two-and-a-half-year-old boys) . . . have you ever witnessed or tried to share with someone deep, heartbreaking sorrow? Kenji's wife grew up in Japan and was therefore Japan-educated. Since marriage, he has been here in Seattle since the early '30s. Coming from a fairly well-to-do family, his wife has really suffered from the sudden move to camp. On top of that, she moved to Puyallup without Kenji, who was here in jail. The two little ones are always asking her, "Where's Daddy? When is he coming back?" Each night the younger one prays, "Please, God, bring Daddy home to see me."

These little intimate things Kenji shares with me in the evenings in our cell. In broken English, his wife writes him vivid letters. He reads them to me, interrupted by several pauses, while he swallows that lump or stifles a sob. The boys think Kenji is in a Boise hotel. Since it was Mr. Stafford who drove him away, the boys always ask him, "When are you bringing Daddy home?" After reading aloud to me, he put away the letters, but he pulls them out often. Quite often I can notice him brushing something off his face. Kenji remarked, "You know I'm a family man; I love my home and family. I'm finding now that the more attached you are to someone, the harder it is for you in cases like this."

I think that is true. As Gibran states, "Joy and sorrow spring from the same reservoir." I hope things will work out all right for Kenji's family and that his wife will not be embittered or become engulfed with hopelessness. "For the sake of the children whom we love, and for me, please take this news chin up. I'm sorry to have caused you so much misery," he wrote his wife. I realized that this was but one unique case of tragedy caused by this war. How many, many more must there be of similar tragedies? It was a long while before I fell asleep.

On Tuesday morning, we had a great deal of excitement. Kenji was told to get his stuff. He was to leave for the "Island" (McNeil Penitentiary). It was very confusing to Kenji because he was supposed to be notified a day in advance. As he had been refused the privilege of phoning his attorney before he got ready to go, I went to the cell with him and helped him pack. We were so stunned by the suddenness of this move that we were nearly overcome with excitement. Hurriedly, Kenji changed his clothes, and while he dressed, he gave me his lawyer's address, his wife's address, and a few other things for me to do after he left. Sadly, we shook hands. In the day tank, several boys ran up to shake hands with him and wish him well. He could not say much. With blankets and setup and his extra things in his hands, he walked out. I sat down with a sigh; I could only reflect and recall some of the wonderful moments we spent together in our cell. And then, about a half hour later, back comes Kenji with all his things. He was able to talk to Lane Summers, and now he won't be going to McNeil for a week or so. Oh, it was wonderful—so unexpected and sudden. Immediately, we got in the game of hearts and tried to throw him the queen. Kenji was happy to stay a while longer with us, as terrible and confining as this place is.

CHAPTER 8

Jail Visitations

KING COUNTY JAIL HAS TWO DAYS A WEEK THAT ARE CALLED visitors' days. The visiting facility is perfectly horrible here, where you can either talk or look, and you have to yell into an inhuman contraption to be heard.

The sheriff said of me, "This boy has more friends than anybody I ever saw." All of those friends were Caucasian, since all my Japanese friends and relatives had been swept into WCCA centers and WRA camps.

For the first time in over two months, I had the opportunity to see many of my friends face-to-face. It's wonderful to be able to talk like decent human beings again. For all the things that I lack, no one can say that I lack friends. I had all sorts of people coming, including Reverend Murphy—the old family standby—my college friends, my defense committee, and my lawyers, in addition to various pals.

I was informed that Floyd Schmoe of the American Friends Service Committee is back in town and is trying to see me. I was surprised to find how happy that news made me. I have always been close to Floyd and respected him, but I did not realize just how close. The very mention of his name cheered me. He is the symbol of effective Christian action—humble love. During his brief trip to the Bay Area, Floyd visited Pinedale camp and my family. I shall look forward to seeing him.

After making arrangements, Floyd Schmoe finally got a permit to see me outside of the regular visiting days. As I was anticipating a face-to-face visit, I was greatly disappointed to find that we had to talk through the attorney's cage. As there was another visitor, all I heard was his voice reverberating in the metal room. Further arrangements were made by my lawyer, Frank Walters, and I hope that the next visit will be decent.

Floyd Schmoe and daughters, Esther and Ruthanna, dropped in this afternoon. . . . Ruthanna was too bashful to speak. She is a peach. In spite of many discouragements, Floyd was able to share encouraging news. The relocation area is such an improvement over the assembly centers. A few students have been released, and there is even a fair chance for families to be released. AFSC isn't leaving any stones unturned.

Esther is mad at me. I am an expert ribber, often to my detriment. As of today she has written me three letters, *but* refuses to mail them on. Shucks, when she mentioned that, I was dumbfounded. I even forgot to mention how lovely and refreshing she looked in her green summer dress. Esther was interested in the possibility of the Quakers conducting religious services here. I could not give her much information. If we had better visiting facilities, I could have told her the reactions to various approaches and some suggestions for a program. The greatest difficulty will be the arrangement or permission to conduct a meeting. I believe a program of interest and friendship will go much further than anything else here.

Last night I was the recipient of a delicious pineapple upside-down cake. It was made and delivered by Donna Hines, my college friend. If more could have seen the way those boys (Kenji, Ted, Ed, Shige, and Tom) went after it and fought over the extra third that was left over, they would think the boys hadn't eaten for a month! Was it delicious!

I was surprised to see Donna. She had just left for California a week ago. I was sorry to see her go. Donna is the inspirational type, deeply sensitive and responsive, and highly original. When she gets in a "mood," she has to act. I feel that instead of suppressing those moods, those sensitive feelings, the thing that should be done is to direct her desires and her actions toward positive channels. Therefore, I encouraged her to go, and go with enthusiasm, and free conscience, and expectancy.

Donna reports a wonderful trip, though short. Her grandmother, now alone since Granddad's recent passing, became almost hysterical at the news of Donny's scooting to San Francisco; so she came home. She will remain with Granny this quarter.

Just before a trip to California via Tule Lake camp, my college friend Ellie came in to see me with her father, Dr. Ring. Local news was brought to the fore, including conditions at the University's Eagleson Hall and International House. She will drop in at Portland for a short while and try to see her friend at the North Portland center; then go to the Tule Lake camp to see the folks, then to Berkeley, where Donna is. The Cascade Locks CO [conscientious objector] camp is also on her itinerary.

Mary Farquharson of my defense committee brought Homer Morris for a visit. We talked a little about last Saturday's appeal, or rather hearing, and then the conversation went along to WCCA center and WRA camp setups. Contrary to Floyd's reactions, Homer Morris thought the WRA camps, outside of the personnel, were not too great an improvement over WCCA centers. Generally rated as the no. 2 man in the American Friends Service Committee and considered by many as the top man in his field (that of resettlement) Morris himself presents a very contrasting picture as an interested, humble layman. I only hope that if I ever become a person of influence in some way that I can maintain that same spirit of humility. It is such a beautiful spirit but so hard to possess.

Little by little, I'm getting to know on an intimate basis the responsible leaders of the American Friends Service Committee. My lawyer, Arthur Barnett, brought in G. Raymond Booth, another humble person who never indicates his position by his attitude. Also there is Caleb Foote, who was born in Cambridge, Massachusetts, and graduated in 1939 from Harvard, where he was the managing editor of the *Harvard Crimson* and earned a master's degree in economics in 1941. The Quaker faith of his mother drew him to pacifism, and Foote was hired in 1941 by the Fellowship of Reconciliation to open its Northern California office.

I had the rare opportunity of visiting with Reverend Nevin Sayre and Bayard Rustin of the Fellowship of Reconciliation. They were in the Northwest on their way to the Pacific Coast FOR convention at Berkeley and also the Pacific Northwest Conference here in Seattle. Reverend Sayre, an Episcopal minister, founded the Episcopal Peace Fellowship. Bayard Rustin is a Quaker, Socialist, and the race relations secretary for the FOR. [A civil rights activist, Rustin worked in California on behalf of the incarcerated Nisei during World War II and later worked with Martin Luther King, Jr.] The visit was not very long, but they are certainly inspiring to me. We closed our meeting, at Bayard's suggestion, with a few moments of silent meditation and a prayer by Reverend Sayre. It was truly one of the most deeply felt and satisfying moments I've had since coming here. I intend to keep in contact with them.

Norman Thomas, the Socialist leader and FOR secretary, and Rufus Jones, a Quaker, writer, philosopher, college professor, and founder of AFSC, also visited me.

I received a wonderful letter from Reverend Sayre. He mentions meeting Mom at Tule after he left here: "She has a beautiful face that moved me as I talked with her. She gave me a white and a pink carnation that she had made out of tissue paper in her hut. She took them out of a vase of paper flowers in a corner of the room that brightened the whole room. I have my two flowers now on my desk in the Fellowship office here. They will remind me of you and your mother and other friends of Japanese ancestry I met in the three camps that I visited on my recent trip."

Letter from Gordon to Esther Schmoe, King County Jail, October 11, 1942:

> Hi freshie! I'm getting a bit wary of your taking Psych I. Don't
> you start getting funny notions and try any experiments on me! I
> remember about four years ago when I took the same course from
> Wilson. Lois was in my class. It was a one o'clock affair, and I used
> to snooze in the back of the room every afternoon except Thursdays
> when we had demonstrations. Psych is really an interesting subject,

although I don't think much of the UW department. I think their style is outmoded, insufficient of satisfaction. They are behaviorists, and do not recognize a soul. Everything, to them, can be explained by conditioning. I guess a lot of things can be explained as conditioned responses, but there are certain things which are beyond that. The idea of God, inner spirit, conscience, cannot be explained by behaviorism.

I have been visited by at least four ministers: Alex Winston of the Unitarian Church, Dr. Goodenough of Wesley, Rev. Peterson of the Madrona Presbyterian, and today I had a pleasant meeting with Dr. Jensen of First Baptist. Dr. Jensen tried to make arrangements so we could visit at the office, but there were too many down there. He is a wonderful person, trying his best to do his mission. I remember our Campus Christian Council banquet last April. He was our main speaker, and his topic was "In Times Like These." As the title indicates, he spoke of the stormy days and how we, the youths, must face them. "It is an opportunity and a privilege to be living now," he stated. During his address, he made a reference to me about the *Times* articles on conscientious objectors. They were joking comments, but he added: "Now, don't think I'm making fun of him; I'm not. In fact, I think like he does and admire his convictions very much."

Today's visit was just a friendly chat. I believe that is why I enjoyed meeting all of these ministers so much—they were so friendly and spoke of their concerns and troubles and joys. No preaching, no Scripture quotations, no Bible lessons. I appreciate these ministers' works. They are doing a lot, and their work requires so much tactfulness. Occasionally, of course, we see disgusting compromises; but, on the whole, those whom I know are "a swell bunch of people."

Shungo and Mitsuko Hirabayashi and Ruth and Floyd Schmoe at the wedding of Gordon Hirabayashi and Esther Schmoe, Spokane, Washington, July 29, 1944. Courtesy of Susan Carnahan

Nobu and Paul Suzuki hosted Gordon and Esther's wedding reception at their home at 1626 E. Pacific Street, Spokane, Washington, July 29, 1944. This is the same house that Gordon, Floyd Schmoe, and the coalition organized by the American Friends Service Committee helped the Suzukis purchase, despite the protests of some Euro-American neighbors. Courtesy of Susan Carnahan

Gordon and Esther Hirabayashi standing outside the Lidgerwood Evangelical Church after their Quaker wedding, Spokane, Washington, July 29, 1944. Courtesy of Susan Carnahan

1945

Season's Greetings

S. Hirabayashi + Family

Hirabayashi family's Christmas card, December 1944. From left, seated on floor: James and Richard. Seated on couch: Shungo, Mitsuko, and Esther. Esther (Tosh) is standing behind the couch. The photo was taken at the family's residence, E. 2012 N. Crescent Avenue, Spokane, Washington. Courtesy of Sharon M. Yuen

CHAPTER 9

World War II Interracial Marriage

[Diary entries from] King County Jail, August 1942— . . .
If more of our so-called love and marriages were based on others' concerns without ulterior motives, this would be a much happier world in which to live, and more people would experience something more closely approximating true love. As it is today, most of us are too busy to be anything but selfish. I know, because I am often that way myself. Even our love is a thing hurried. . . . I think life is an art. . . . There must be a purpose, a center, and a balance. . . . There must be depth. There must be color and contrasts. There must be the subtlety of suggestion. . . . There must be room for growth. In short there must be harmony. . . . The most powerful of the divine qualities is love. Love is our most aggressive spirit—love is our most patient—love is the basis of our greatest joy—love is the spring of our deepest sorrows—love is our best healer—love is the most forgiving spirit and, therefore, the most creative force. With a glimpse of love through experience, one finally approaches that harmony—that symphony of life.

King County Jail, November 1942—Last night, feeling alone and solitary, I became reflective and meditative. . . . I thought of the days when I shall again be out, working for a period with the Service Committee, then back to get my degree. . . . I tried to picture our future. . . . As we talked, I began to see why you always bobbed up. It's the way you live—you're always getting into somebody's life. If it isn't the COs—it's the evacuees . . . or it's maybe anybody needing a friend. Has anyone called you an altruist? . . . Sometimes I can't imagine anyone being so selfless, and so natural about it . . . try to live like you and your folks. . . . Have you selected a hospital yet? Swedish Hospital is the best for good nurses along private and hospital duty. . . . For public health work and things along the line of AFSC, Harborview Hospital is the best training ground. . . . I like your attitude in regards to service and sacrificial sharing, it is beautiful. . . . I may be able to grasp the spirit.

September 1943, on the way from Spokane, Washington, to Weiser, Idaho—I sat on the baggage, waiting for cars, doing a bit of meditating and reflecting. Things that are ordinarily overlooked are viewed in their proper perspective . . . even the stars seemed beyond approach but yet within comprehension; they seemed to be viewing the feverish ways of man with "When will he ever learn?" I looked up and talked to our star, the brightest of the triangle near the Dipper: "Dear star, will you always keep close to the real values of life? . . . Will you bring me the charm that will bring understanding to others . . . of the beauties and the fullness of real living?"

Want to hear a good one? Mom thought you had already given me the brush-off. She said she thought it was only a youthful fancy of yours. When I told her we thought often of marriage before you receive your registered nurse's degree, she seemed a little pleased in addition to being a little surprised. I guess she thinks it's impossible for a guy like me to hold a girl like you!

October 1943—Among my friends here in the Tucson jail, one goes with a Jewish girl and another goes with an Armenian girl. We had a wonderful discussion on intermarriage. We all agreed on the true basis for all marriages—mutual love based upon selfless concerns. . . . I have seen into the future of our lives . . . you told of your hopes and plans for marriage this June. . . . The life of the future will be a life of constant strain—physically, mentally, emotionally, spiritually. . . . Knowledge of physiology, neurology, and the various therapies will really be useful. I want to get as much training in this field as possible.

You can help me, of course . . . , we have growth and plans for a year or two in China. . . .

April 1944—Your mother wrote indicating three abnormalities: a long engagement, a separated married life, giving up school. . . .

June 1944—Say, couldn't we be married in Seattle, Quaker style? Think the Quakers would approve? . . . If it is too embarrassing for the Quakers to plan for our wedding unless I'm in Seattle legitimately with the heavenly authority, i.e., the Western Defense Command, then we'll be married over here in Spokane. . . . I'm going to Seattle next month, but I'm coming over like a decent human being and not a criminal that has to have a permit and an escort. . . . On consideration, I feel we should be married in Spokane; that is the halfway point for both our parents. Another reason is that if something should happen to me in Seattle, the papers would really give the intermarriage angle the royal works. . . . I have always pictured Quaker weddings as the simple thing as opposed to some of the more elaborate church weddings. . . .

From FBI files, *Washington Star* (Associated Press), July 2, 1944:

ACCUSED JAP-AMERICAN TO MARRY QUAKER GIRL

Gordon K. Hirabayashi . . . has obtained a marriage license application form in Spokane to wed an American girl. The bride to be is Miss Esther Schmoe, 20, former University of Washington student and daughter of Floyd Schmoe, who said: "We haven't disapproved of the engagement. We have a great deal of admiration for this boy. If they are getting married now, it is their own affair, and they have our blessings."

July 25, 1944—I was rather perturbed that our wedding was growing into such a large and public affair, but now I am reconciled to it . . . this will be the first Quaker ceremony in this town, I believe, and this will be the first marriage of people with a somewhat different racial origin. We have much to offer and a responsibility to encourage others to live the life of brotherhood. . . . Life is really empty and nothing if service and fellowship both inspired from Spirit are absent. Our marriage ceremony should be symbolic of our life. The friends who shall witness our event will represent all races of mankind, and we shall endeavor to continue our widening circle of friends.

From FBI files, *St. Paul Dispatch*, August 2, 1944:

> Spokane (AP)—Miss Esther Schmoe and Gordon Hirabayashi, Japanese American youth who gained nationwide attention by bringing a test suit challenging government evacuation orders, were married Saturday. . . .

Even after my sentence, the press included the fact that I had married a Caucasian.

CHAPTER 10

Prison Meditations

PURSUING HIS STUDY OF NEGRO-OWNED NEWSPAPERS, WEST-
brook Pegler notes that some few are "excited about the arbitrary
deportation of Japanese and native Americans of Japanese ancestry from military areas of the Pacific Coast" (June 4, 1942; quoted in
"Views & Views," George S. Schuyler, *Los Angeles Negro Daily*, 6 June
1942). Pegler quotes from two who ask why citizens of German and
Italian ancestry have not been similarly deported. He alleged that
"some American natives of Japanese birth were traitorous spies who
helped a treacherous enemy slaughter our people at Pearl Harbor and
that many [Nisei] children were educated by their parents to be Japanese, not Americans." He excuses the government's drastic tearing up
of the Bill of Rights in this instance by citing its "alarm or fear and
military urgency."

REGARDING RACISM

Negroes and Indians have often been run off their land and penned
in virtual concentration camps. This is the first instance in modern
American history of enforced mass migration. The Founding Fathers
clearly saw the possible dangers, and they erected the safeguard of
the Bill of Rights and the Civil War amendments as protection against
such arbitrary actions. It is the evil from which the European ancestors of our present patriots fled. If this is to be the new order here,
then the war is already lost so far as democracy is concerned.

What evidence is there that Japanese residents or citizens of Nipponese ancestry constituted any "dangerous military problem" except in the minds of alarmists? None whatsoever. In contrast to these largely peaceful and patriotic Japanese are the Italian Americans with their numerous Fascist leagues and the German Americans with their bunds. It seems to me that all of these Nazi-Fascists should be incarcerated rather than citizens against whom no charges of disloyalty can be substantiated. Pegler declares that deporting all Americans of Italian and German ancestry would cripple our army, navy, and war industries. But is that a sound reason for discriminating against Japanese Americans? Is there any basis for this except a racial one?

I think the average intelligent Negro confronted with the "problem" on the Pacific Coast would have told the prejudiced white competitors of the Japanese Americans to go jump in the sea. Guided himself by the Bill of Rights, he would have assumed every citizen to be innocent until proven guilty, regardless of color. If the Constitution can be tossed aside expediently whenever those in authority choose, then democracy is already dead and our struggle on its behalf is pointless.

REGARDING DEMOCRACY

President Franklin D. Roosevelt, June 4, 1942—"We are fighting as our fathers have tonight, to uphold the doctrine that all men are created equal in the sight of God."

July 4th, 1942, King County Jail—One hundred and sixty-six years ago today, a band of earnest and far-seeing individuals drafted and signed a document: the Declaration of Independence.

Because of their vision and conviction, we, the people of these United States, have made tremendous advancements in the liberation of mankind from political, social, economic, and religious slavery. There are yet many bridges to cross, many highways to build and to travel. We have only begun our quest toward the realization of the free expressions of man and life.

Even in our progress, we have had our ups and downs. We often lapse, even openly, into economic totalitarianism. We have had political, economic, and social discrimination against the Negroes since their beginnings here. In spite of constitutional guarantees, greed, selfishness, and insecurity lead us to fall short in the practice.

Today, in our remembrance of the Day of Independence, there is a dark shadow signifying our shortcomings. Through hysteria and the spread of war psychosis, 113,000 people of "Japanese descent, both alien and non-alien" are confined behind barbed wire and armed guards as prisoners of war. Notice how they are classified—"both alien and non-alien"—a total and deliberate evasion of the recognition that over 60 percent of those confined are native-born American citizens of respectable standing. Descent has taken priority over citizenship. American citizens are being held prisoners by their own government. They are told that to be prisoners is the patriotic thing to do. What shattering of their democratic vision, what a jolt to their social and psychological status as citizens. Tragedy of tragedies, their only crime is that of descent.

But even though this is America, these things happening today are not American. They are the results of misinterpretations, mis-emphasis concerning the right thing to do, hysteria, and short-sightedness. It is up to those of us who feel that a wrong has been committed, that we have fallen short, to bear witness to that fact. It is our obligation to show forth our light in times of darkness, nay, our privilege.

The risk is great, the consequences unpleasant. But there is the vision of those seekers of independence. We must carry the torch. We must live our lives. Fascism must be extinguished here.

Just a rambling thought in remembrance of the 4th—"Incarceration of liberty."

REGARDING RELIGION

August 30, 1942—Lately, I have been delving into quite a bit of Quaker history and philosophy. I have come to understand much better the bases for our belief and faith. In reading John Woolman's journal, I am constantly amazed that one person can put into words so simply and beautifully the description of the spirit that moves him to action. John Woolman is truly a remarkable personality.

Woolman's concern, so deep and sincere, for the plight of the Negro slaves moved him to travel quite extensively from New England to North Carolina. In this respect, I find much similarity between Woolman and Floyd Schmoe. Because of Floyd's deep and sincere concern for the plight of the Japanese people, he has traveled up and down the West Coast, and even over to Hawaii. He has practiced no end of personal sacrifice for their benefit. And like Woolman when he says, "We were sometimes in much weakness, and labored under discouragements, and at other times, through the renewed manifestations of divine love, we had sessions of refreshment wherein the powers of truth prevailed." I'm sure Floyd had many periods of "low visibility" as well as moments of triumph, and always the triumphant overshadowed and eclipsed the low.

When I think of the inspiration I received by acquainting myself with Quaker background as well as Quaker contemporary and the zest for better living it gives me, I wonder what I had been doing all these years oblivious of the Quakers. Perhaps I was groping, searching.

From the journal *The Friend*—The Quaker Soul: "The quickening of the seeker's heart leads to enduring peace as he obeys God's leadings. The inward Christ roots out that which is selfish, impels us to share our brother's suffering, and leads us into that which brings unity and peaceful relationships. Such a peace has been a healing in our Society today. Our hope lies in a new upsurge of power in our meetings, in small devotional groups and in wider fellowship. No matter how difficult the situation before us, if we are owned by the active power of the Lord at all times, we find that we belong to the Kingdom of God, and that we really trust the Lord in every situation."

I received a package from Homer and Edna Morris. I discovered to my great joy that enclosed was a copy of T.R. Kelly's *A Testament of Devotion*. On the front page they wrote that they wanted to share with me the thoughts of the late Kelly, a personal friend of theirs.

Have read the short biographical sketch written by Douglas Steere.

What a full and searching life that man had. From time to time, as I read the thoughtful stimulating articles, I intend to record my reactions.

Lin Yutang in *Between Tears and Laughter*—"I must say that materialists must continue to fight wars eternally. Materialists cannot end wars or devise a peace. They have not the brains for it. Materialists have not the courage to hope. They are not hoping now."

REGARDING PACIFISM

Dr. Thomas, the brother of Norman Thomas (Socialist candidate for president), was not in politics but was a very solid person in terms of his convictions. Even when he agreed to serve as a U.S. Public Health official during World War I, he defended working for the government in wartime on the grounds that what he was doing had universal implications. Norman Thomas was a well-known pacifist and Socialist. He ran for mayor of New York City and president of the U.S. Being an articulate person, he debated on panels with outstanding specialists, making me feel sorry for his opponents because of his debating skills.

So I heard Norman Thomas speak many times but didn't get to meet him on a one-to-one basis until 1942 when he came to see me in the King County Jail. I was also visited by Bayard Rustin, an African American, Quaker, Socialist, and civil rights activist. Well, he was one articulate speaker, in great demand at student conferences. I knew him quite well because he was in a number of leadership seminars. He took positions on his draft status and had spent time as a prisoner as well. In other words, he spoke from personal experience.

While in King County Jail, I also received a letter from George Yamada, a Nisei pacifist, from the CPS camp at Cascade Locks, Oregon. An order, obviously race discrimination hiding under the cloak of the all-inclusive title "Civilian Exclusion Order," called for his removal from the camp so that he could be placed in a "War Relocation Center." As George says, his acceptance would be his permission to the government to practice race prejudice.

On Monday afternoon my discharge order came to the director, Mark Schrock. I expressed my unwillingness to comply. If necessary I am willing to go to an eastern CPS camp.

Schrock tendered his resignation to the Brethren Service Committee and the Selective Service the next day, telling them he would not sign the discharge papers. Letters and telegrams were sent expressing the reaction of the camp. The support, almost 100 percent which has come from the camp, is a source of strength to me, but I had been preparing myself for this emergency for many months and was not surprised at the turn of events. The men have been discussing non-violent techniques to combat this measure.

Fifty men went on an all-day fast on the day following the order. I am not sure of what will happen, but come what may I am willing to pay the price of my faith. Not a few men will support me to the bitter end, so in a way this is a cooperative venture. If I am evacuated I would like to work with you on this whole issue.

George is right. This is a problem bigger than "you or I or just one racial minority." I have felt that all along. This is a question close to the hearts of all Americans and all those interested in the survival of the democratic way, the American way. The inalienable rights of human beings are being grossly neglected. The Christian principle of one Father, and, therefore, the brotherhood of mankind, is denied. The democratic ideal of equality regardless of race, color, or previous condition of servitude is scrapped and forgotten. The basic fundamentals that gave this country the impetus to grow and prosper are rapidly being trampled and abused. George is denied religious freedom to follow the dictates of his conscience. George is denied the privileges of American citizenship due him. The same is true of all Nisei. And what is the underlying reason? Biological descent! That has taken precedence over everything we understand and value, or that is written as guarantees in our Constitution,

The day I went to court to have my trial date set, Jack Merner, a YMCA colleague, came up to see me. It was Jack's farewell to me as he was leaving for Yale Divinity School that afternoon. What really interested me were the courses he was going to take: Religion in Higher Education, Old Testament History and Literature, Theory of Religious Education, Content of the English Bible, and Boys' Work Practicum. What interesting-sounding and stimulating subjects! I feel ambitious and studious just to glance at those subjects. I think I'll do a little studying on my own in terms of the New and Old Testaments.

Jack writes that it is pretty difficult to justify being there, and I can appreciate his feelings. However, his alternative to divinity school was a CPS camp. And of the two, I can't very conscientiously encourage fellows to pick CPS. I don't believe merely in sacrificing, that is, sacrificing in itself. Therefore, when in a previous meeting he had asked my opinion, I said I couldn't really find much difference in the status of 4-D and 4-E classifications.

Bill Makino writes:

Another example of army inconsistency. I got my draft question-naire yesterday. This country seems to be the only place in the world where guys in concentration camps get army notices. Maybe if I were a conscientious objector, my beefs would be perfect. But I just am not. Conscientiously, I feel that, evil as war is, I must do my bit to defeat the Axis powers. I am well aware that I am not a member of any decent democracy, nor would I feel that I was fighting a war for freedom. It's a struggle for survival, as I see it. I'm still "naive" enough to believe that if we build up the proper forces within ourselves during this period of hatred, we can establish a just and durable peace. Maybe I am a fool, but that's the only way I see it.

I think that that is a wonderful statement coming from a fellow who has earnestly sought "the way," even as you and I. The spirit with which he approaches the issue as well as the goal he desires are both things that I admire and adhere to. But to me, to my way of logic, his statement is a series of inconsistencies and contradictions.

For instance, to what avail our defeat of the Axis powers if in the process we ourselves become indoctrinated with their practices and principles? For how can we defeat them in this war but through building a superior military machine? I hate to even think of a more ruthless, more violent, more destructive, more vicious—in short, superior—military machine than that of the Axis powers. Can we ever hope for democracy in the hands of such a power? For labor? For survival? Are we so good that if we are defeated, the world is doomed? Are we defeated if we are militarily second best? How could Jesus ever accept the cross if he felt his death and removal would mean doom for the people, all of whom he loved? Isn't it strange how that very cross is the symbol of our Christian faith? I'm not so sure mere survival is worth the price involved in war with its multitude of sacrifices.

The crux of his whole statement is that word *if* in the clause "if we build up the proper forces. . . ." If that "if" holds true, then I myself can accept Bill's statement. But believing in the old adage that "the means determine the ends," and feeling that means and ends are inseparable and must be consistent, I cannot put much faith in that "if."

The only way to pierce darkness, to overcome it, is not by a darker darkness or more of it. There must be light. In the same way, we cannot build within ourselves proper forces for a just and durable peace by cooperating and participating in the very forces that instigate hate, distrust, suspicion, prejudice, totalitarian attitudes. Love is the only thing powerful enough to overcome hate, suspicion, and so forth. Love is the only thing that develops and nurtures personalities.

A Christian pacifist refuses cooperation in war efforts, but only because he or she believes in and participates in a different and what he or she considers to be a more positive, a more certain, way of developing that trust and understanding among people. That is essential to any just and durable peace.

One more Nisei has joined the ranks of delinquents. Kenji Okuda (University YMCA) said that he has returned his Nisei questionnaire unfilled-out to his Seattle board. He mentioned that John Swomley told him about my actions, which led him to study and examine the situation very closely. After due consideration, he came to the conclusion that he couldn't enlist and joined my ranks. Ken will work for the FOR this summer, speaking on the Nisei situation.

Although previously, I was in the 4-E class and prepared to go to

CPS camp, but now I am clear in my mind that I can accept neither 4-E nor any other classification. I oppose conscription, and were I given another opportunity, I would never register for it. It is too late to backtrack about what I did on October 16, 1940, but now I feel that I must dissociate myself as far and as clearly as I can from the bonds of conscription. I know it will mean several years in prison, but were I called again, I know my course. The Selective Service System had ordered me to a conscientious objectors camp, but I have moved on to another position beyond. If I was opposed to war, I'd be opposed to the Selective Service System, so I wouldn't want anything to do with it. A kind of radical position, "absolutist" during the wartime period.

There was an interesting conversation going on in the next cell last night. They were discussing the international situation. Ha! I thought it was rich—a group of young fellows incarcerated as draft violators (failure to keep in touch with the draft board). The consensus seemed to be that Japan was underestimated in power; that they don't care to fight for England or Australia; that if the U.S. perfected her own defenses, no nation could conquer her; that they would prefer being defense workers, even cowards rather than dead heroes. It was quite a session. Anything under the sun is discussed in this place.

If you could think of churches that believed in the Prince of Peace and the Catholic Church, I ran into a Catholic conscientious objector in prison. He was rejected by his church. They had stars for each of their members who were in the military. This guy was disowned for taking the stand that you could reach from statements that the Catholics say they believe in, and so he couldn't participate in the military: "I can't do it that way, I feel, being a good Catholic." So he was in prison.

Something must have happened to the letter I received from Howie. It was dated September 8 and postmarked September 9, yet I received the letter October 8. No marks were on the envelope or the letter. Perhaps it was investigated or inspected secretly. Something seems phony.

It was a fine letter, and I'm sorry it was delayed so long in getting to me. Howie states that he is prepared to leave the CO camp and work on a farm near where Ruane lives. He is interested in learning the "rudiments of farming and search out a philosophy of intentional living more and more." He knows such a plan will not attract many of the "socially significant" but feels there is something in that. "This will be an experiment in living functionally, on a subsistence level."

Howie is interested in the way of life and teaching of Jesus. I do not know exactly why, but Jesus seemed to teach through personal example, and he always worked from the personal angle. Howie feels the same way, "for how can we change nations if the peoples within are not willing to change?" I think Howie's right—at least, I am in agreement with him.

Changes, he feels, need not start from anything that was. It can start anew, revolutionary. And that is where principles, courage of conviction, and discipline (an inner discipline) are needed. Compromises are destructive. . . . An action compromised induces weaker-minded ones to follow suit on the strength of that compromise. Consequences may affect, but should not alter, the principle.

Another point Howie brings out is that maybe man's duty is not to eradicate even the basest wrongs. Yet, even so, he himself should wash his hands clean and no longer support or actively engage in that which he considers wrong.

Such teachings of Jesus as "Resist not evil," "Whosoever shall smite thee on the right cheek, turn him the other also," "Love your enemies," "Take no thought of the morrow, for the morrow shall take thoughts for the things of itself," "Sell what thou hast and give to the poor" seem contradictory to intelligence and survival. And here comes Howie again with "That is just the point! Jesus did not expect this world to survive. The only hope for survival lies in doing the things not of this world but of the ideal world. And today is the time to begin, lest tomorrow be too late."

His letter shows evidence of much thought and meditation, and I am enriched through sharing his ideas with him. I do not know what the consequences of his refusal to stay in camp will be, but I am not afraid for him.

Not so long ago, his wife, Ruane, sent me a wonderful letter. It seems she will be teaching in a very progressive Friends elementary school. This school, just organized, is the result of the concerns of Quaker parents who were worried about their offspring's education. This newly organized school is based on the work camp idea, with children making their own lunches as part of their education. In this manner, they will learn something about diet, cleanliness, balance, arithmetic, and so forth.

Ruane is a good friend for Howie, giving him much strength and inspiration. She writes: "We are finding a compelling drive within, to seek Truth, Gordie. To be true to those convictions within, without compromise, is all important. It seems essential that we make known to others what we believe to be true, and by that, so live. 'Seek ye first the Kingdom' has gained a new impetus for me; it becomes all consuming."

She says she looks forward to the day, "someday somewhere," when I can come down and live with them for a while. "Surely, sometime such will be possible, if even for a short period."

I say the desire is mutual, and someday I will have a good sharing of experiences with them. How things have changed, and how Howie and I have matured since our college roommate days.

In October 1940, Howard and I had both been classified 1-A. Howard's draft board denied his request for conscientious objector status, deciding that his religious argument was based more on humanist principles than on theology. We both had to appeal and received our 4-E conscientious objector classifications in 1941. We thought we would be going to one of those conscientious objectors' camps. This alternative was known as Civilian Public Service. Because of my ancestry, I was barred from such service. Howard, however, was sent to a CPS camp in Southern California.

REGARDING THE WAR RELOCATION AUTHORITY CAMPS

An airmail from the family says that packing and preparation for a transfer is now under way. . . . Mother says she had to crawl under the bed on the cement to get something resembling relief. . . . She did

not know if the new place will be better or worse; however, she is prepared to "take it," come what may. Boy, that's real spirit! Kid brother
Ed wrote:

> Hotter'n Hell
> Work like Hell
> Felt like Hell
> Look like Hell
> So why shouldn't
> I go to Hell?

Mother wrote that daily, early every morning and late each evening since she left Auburn, she looks at the North Star and talks to
me. Then she closes each session with a prayer. It seems silly in a way
to do all that, but I could not prevent a big lump from flirting with my
throat. She's a real trouper, as good as they come. She told me about
her gray hairs, claiming that I was the cause of most of them. Well, it's
true. I've really raised havoc with her life with my unorthodox way of
life and continually getting into trouble of some kind even though it
is always trouble of the impersonal type. Time and again, she would
worry herself sick, then reproach me from every angle. When I refuse
to change, she turns around and becomes my strongest supporter.
Wonder if all mothers are like that? I hope I can show her before it's
too late that I realize she's all right.

An excited report from Tule Lake reveals plans for Eddie to leave
camp for the sugar beet fields of Utah. "Just a first step out," says Ed.
"A step toward becoming a free man," was Mom's hopeful comment.

The relief in Mother's hopeful comments is encouraging. She con-
fessed that Ed, not I, had taken the front seat as far as she is concerned. After Ed leaves for Utah, he hopes to move on to a better job
or, if fortunate, to a school (college). Most of the group with whom he
is leaving expect to return when the season is over—"but yours truly
ain't doin' any returnin'," Ed emphatically writes. I sincerely hope and
pray that this move will mean not only Ed's entrance into fairly normal life again but also the opening wedge for the rest of the family.

That being so will, of course, mean that thousands of others will be leaving camp soon also.

The most decent, far-seeing, positive thing that those interested in the welfare of these evacuees, and the evacuees themselves, can do is to work toward the release from these places of internment. The sooner, the better.

Ted Takahashi writes in his first letter that there is a lot to be done in the camps. So far, his life had been one of "shaking hands each step I take, no matter where it is: outside, in the shower room, the mess hall, or the toilet." Ted is very much disappointed with the internal disorder and dissension in camp. The JACL Nisei leaders are nothing but Jackson Street kids and drunk with power, as he put it. The food, the visiting privileges, and the hospital are some of the things that operated peculiarly and mysteriously. Well, I hope the move from Puyallup to Minidoka means a new order of some kind. The evacuees' morale can't go much lower.

Kenji Iki wrote concerning Ted Takahashi's visit to camp. He doesn't know if the authorities have loosened up to allow him in or his visit was merely another rumor. Both of these fellows are doing splendid work. They are brilliant fellows, concerned about humanity, and doing their best to make life more meaningful to their fellow evacuees. Both are living Christians and shall be a contribution to society. I gain much from their fellowship and am glad to be included as their friend.

Through Kenji Iki, I had a good description—an insider's description of Puyallup (Camp Harmony) and Idaho. Puyallup was really a nightmare: graft and injustice on the part of both the incompetent WCCA officials and the inexperienced, misguided JACL officers. Food was terrible, largely because the cooks were former "Skid Road" restaurant operators and were still following the same approach. No one knows where the $800 appropriated for recreation went. Internal camp management was horribly mishandled. Petty politics and selfish ambitions were two other factors—major factors—in the lack of harmony at Camp Harmony.

On the other hand, the WRA camp in Idaho (Minidoka) shows a

lot of promise, largely because of the infinitely higher-quality staff. When Kenji Iki was called to Seattle to be indicted, Mr. Stafford, the director of the WRA camp, drove him 150 miles to Baker. During four hours or so of driving, Kenji felt he had the rarest privilege of talking frankly about the problems both faced. It seems Stafford has an inkling of the cause of disunity at Puyallup and has the ability to size individuals up. At any rate, he intends to have democracy and self-government prevail, and after an interview with Clarence Arai (a Nisei leader), he'd pretty accurately sized Kenji up. Under his regime, it seems evacuees will have no trouble leaving camp, as long as they can guarantee work or sponsors outside. If Kenji's impressions are correct, Stafford seems to be the perfect man for that job. Kenji feels that Eden will grow into the richest town in Idaho. He maintains that with proper facilities and proper management, a rich agricultural community will develop. If those communities will develop and be under the same status as any other town, like those Amish and other communities back in Pennsylvania and elsewhere, I shall be greatly relieved.

It is too bad a person like Kenji couldn't have been left to contribute to the development of Minidoka. The law moved him here; Masuda, Ito, and others were removed by petty politics. Kenji's advice to Stafford was that a gross mistake will be carried out if too much responsibility is placed on the shoulders of the youth and the inexperienced. It is well-grounded advice.

CHAPTER 11

Pretrial

TWO SIGNIFICANT THINGS HAPPENED THIS WEEK (JULY 4, 1942) that were of interest from the legal side. First, my lawyer, Frank Walters, came in with a plea of abatement. This plea stated that I was a native-born citizen of good standing and, as such, should receive the benefits thereof. Therefore, I should not be incarcerated any longer but should be released immediately. The hearing for this plea will come on July 13. It is very doubtful that the judge will do other than refuse to accept it. I presume that will lead to the trial. Inasmuch as citizenship is completely ignored, I feel this plea is a wise legal move.

On Monday, July 13, I was due in court for the hearing on the plea for abatement. However, as U.S. Attorney Hile was out of town, it was postponed until Friday. Friday came along, found me all dressed and shaved, but I waited in vain. No one came for me. As ordinary, I dressed in my plain clothes on Saturday morn. The door opened and I heard, "Gordon, get ready for court in fifteen minutes!" In haste, I dressed and soon was on my way to the U.S. Court building with Deputy Marshal Jim Bridges. We walked. Pleasant walk, sans handcuffs. The marshal was in a very talkative mood; he seemed to be very sympathetic with our predicament and voiced opinions on Ito, Masuda, and the Takahashi cases. On the elevator going up, I ran into my university friend Eleanor Ring. She came to my hearing. What a pleasant surprise! Gossiped rapidly. She had a different hairdo, and it took a second before I recognized her. Very becoming!

Frank Walters had prepared a trial brief of sixteen pages. It was wonderfully written, involving a lot of research and analysis. He had denounced both the evacuation and curfew orders as unconstitutional and void, Public Law 503 as too vague, etc. Case after case was cited as precedent. Walters quoted Daniel Webster's definition of due process of law, "a law which hears before it condemns, proceeds upon inquiry, and renders judgment only after trial." Of course, that was not the case with either evacuation or curfew. The president, as commander in chief during wartime, has powers vested in him to exercise against certain people as protection and precaution against sabotage or espionage. Those certain people are all natives, citizens, denizens, or subjects of the hostile nation or government. This includes all persons fourteen years of age and upward, all persons not actually naturalized. These people are liable to be apprehended, restrained, secured, and removed as alien enemies. Nisei are not included in those classes. But they are. In the case of evacuation, the category "alien enemies" was diminished for Germans and Italians (they are still at large), while it was increased for all persons of Japanese ancestry, citizens or otherwise.

U.S. Attorney Hile's arguments were few and, to my way of thinking, evaded the issues brought up. He maintained this was not confinement but merely an exclusion. It was a natural military step and necessary. (1) What if Nisei were allowed to remain where they were and Japanese parachute troops landed? How are we to distinguish? (2) It is for their own protection, that we are putting them in protective custody.

Frank Walters made a very appropriate and significant statement when he said to the judge, Lloyd Black, "to paraphrase what Jesus said, 'What gains a man when he wins the whole world and loses his soul?' What gains America if she wins a military victory and loses the Constitution?"

Judge Black made a few insignificant statements. I believe he likes to sound off and sound important. At any rate, Black felt that the Constitution ought to be flexible enough to be able to protect itself. We are at war, and engaged in a war, the magnitude of which we had never before seen. Therefore we have to take certain measures we feel are necessary for the successful prosecution of that war. The judge also read a previous decision he had made on a similar case. At the present time, he still maintains his previous opinion and added, "The defense has not only to show their points before an open-minded judge but must convince a judge to change his present opinion, which, I admit, is a rather difficult thing to do." So we did not ask for a hurried decision; it will be given later. I can guess the decision, but will he feel fit to give it?

On October 8, I met an FBI agent at the jail office. He was interested in knowing where my parents were staying now. I told him I didn't feel at liberty to speak to him without first consulting my attorney. This agent assured me that he had already met Mr. Walters, and he had said it was okay. However, as I was not satisfied, we called him on the phone. Mr. Walters felt that the D.A. wanted to bring one of my parents up to testify of their birth in Japan. He also felt no reason not to cooperate at this point, so, agreeing, I told the FBI man my parents' correct address.

I have a feeling that the government has more reason than that to go to the trouble of bringing one of my parents here. I was asked which of my parents I would rather have come to this trial. I felt my mother would make a better witness, but I was not sure of her emotional status. Frank Walters contacted Mary Farquharson and then phoned back. It was her suggestion that I have whichever parent I wanted to see the most. After considering it, the likelihood that whoever came up would stay at this jail, the various questions that would be asked, etc., I decided that Mother should come up. There happens to be another Issei lady (from Minidoka) serving a twelve-month sentence in the women's tank here, and that might give Mom an opportunity to feel a little more comfortable here than would otherwise be the case. If Dad were brought up, he would probably he kept apart from me, being a government witness, and therefore would feel alone. Then, too, because of her reading habits, Mom is more informed, I think. I wrote Mom immediately of the new development, giving her as much dope as I could, and adding that it would be wonderful to see her again. I do hope the trip will not upset her, especially the stay in jail. But then, she may welcome an opportunity to share some of my plight in a physical sense, in addition to the mental and spiritual sharing. Also, I think Mom will be of cheer to this lady already in jail on a bribery charge. Anyway, I shall keep my fingers crossed and hope for the best.

While they were in the marshal's office yesterday, my fellow Nisei inmates overheard that some twelve or fifteen witnesses were to be subpoenaed for my trial. Two were scheduled to come from Tule Lake and two from Minidoka. One will undoubtedly be my mother. I wonder who the others can be? Also to be subpoenaed are Floyd Schmoe and Ellie Ring. Helen Blom and Ralph Eaton will probably be included in that list, too. All of these people will be asked about my curfew violations. I have a hunch Arthur Barnett, my legal advisor, will be subpoenaed, too. I am sure none of these persons minds going to the stand. However, I'm sorry to have them called and asked to go through possible embarrassment. And the funny part is that none of these people would have been involved had I not kept a diary, or if I hadn't brought it along to jail, where the FBI picked it up. Maybe it isn't so funny after all. For the witnesses and for myself, we should have nothing to fear. Merely state the truth.

One evening, shortly before my October trial, Kenji Iki and I had finished looking at the *Seattle Times* and *Post-Intelligencer* and had talked for some time. Around 12:30, we were both quiet; I was just dozing off. The night guard came down the hall followed by a "Japanesy" fellow. They stopped by my cell, and the guard asked, "You know this fellow?"

"Nope," and I looked to see if Kenji knew him. As Kenji stretched his neck for a look, I took a more awake observation. In a subdued exclamation, I said, "Hey, that's my dad!"

When the guard went back and opened the door, we pulled him in, fixed his bunk, talked for about an hour. Then we all started snoozing; only I was awake thinking about various things until about 4 a.m.

Unbeknownst to me, the government had subpoenaed both of my parents as witnesses from the Tule Lake concentration camp in California. This was presumably to establish the fact that they were from Japan and that I was their son and therefore of Japanese ancestry, making me subject to the curfew and exclusion proclamations. It was really preposterous. I had never denied my origins but had steadfastly maintained that ancestry did not constitute a crime or indicate a tendency to commit one. Moreover, as an American, I argued that my citizenship was guaranteed by the Constitution regardless of race, creed, color, or national origin. I felt it grossly callous of the government to subpoena my parents as witnesses and then put them in jail. Of course, not even a harmless God-fearing couple of Japanese descent could obtain a hotel room or other public accommodations at that time. My legal team told me later that they had tried to get the government's permission to lodge my parents privately. When the officials balked, my lawyers then proposed that the owners of the designated home be deputized, and thus my parents would be technically in custody. The officials refused this suggestion, and that's how my dad wound up in my jail cell.

The following afternoon, the captain arranged it so I could meet Mom. She was just getting over the effects of the car ride from Tule Lake. They left camp about 8:30 a.m. and arrived in Seattle around midnight. She was in "bed" all day today. I was surprised to see how thin she's become. As I walked up to her, she was sitting in the office, in a dark dress, quietly. Tears trickled down her cheeks, but she soon overcame her emotions. We talked for over an hour. She seemed kind of proud that I didn't go to camp after all. She spoke quite normally, but I failed to see the jolly, peppy Mom I used to know. Her eyes were full of sorrow. Her features were chiseled by sadness and suffering. A melancholy beauty, I sadly reflected.

I don't think it's proper for the federal government to call two witnesses to town and then keep them in jail. I think they should be accorded either a hotel room or a private home or sent back to Tule. They tried to make Mom wear the prison green. She refused. When they insisted, she told them she was a witness and shouldn't stay there in the first place. She asked to call my attorney; then the matron left her alone. Gee, I was proud to hear that! But it pains me terribly. I must leave no stone unturned for their removal to a better place.

There was a silver lining. I had five wonderful days of visiting with my father before the trial and another five days after that. But I was concerned about Mom. I do not at all relish the idea of her being here in jail. There was only one women's tank, whether it was city, state, or federal offense, so there were streetwalkers, shoplifters, embezzlers, and the like. Yet if she is brought to my trial, such will be her fate. Knowing how she feels about jails, I wanted so much to avoid this. But I am so helpless. It is things like this that hurt me most. Mom has gone through a lot these past twenty-five years or so, particularly in the past few months. Through it all, she has emerged tired and worn, but triumphant. I have no fear of her spirit breaking at this point. I only hope that she will be spared as much as possible additional sorrows.

When Mom came to my trial, she was in the women's tank. There was a piano there, a rundown one, and not all of the keys were working. Mom walked around. Everybody was in clusters of twos or threes; nobody paid any attention to her. Mom's not the type to get immediately intimidated. She saw the piano, so she plunked it a little bit. Nobody was paying attention, so she sat down and played a few tunes. And people started to gather around and they started singing. When the whole bunch gathered around, she got a little embarrassed. "Oh, I can't play anymore. Someone else play."

And they said, "No, play some more. Nobody plays here. You're the only one." And they forced her to play, and some of them were singing with tears coming down.

On the day of the trial, she was late making an appearance because six women prisoners decided to give her a royal beauty treatment, including hairstyling, a facial, and a manicure. She came looking like . . . a queen! Until this visit, my parents had worried about my physical condition. No more! While they noted that the tank was cockroach-infested and the food greasy, they also learned that the inmates were warm, friendly people. Moreover, I was the mayor of my tank. Nothing I wrote in letters alleviated their concerns about my well-being really as much as their trip to Seattle under federal subpoena.

CHAPTER 12

Seattle Federal District Court

FRANK WALTERS, RETAINED BY THE GORDON HIRABAYASHI Defense Committee as chief counsel, was the second lawyer hired. The first was John Geisness, a young, bright lawyer in a large firm that represented the Teamsters Union. The union had objected: "We're not happy that a firm representing us is taking the Hirabayashi case." The union would not be able to retain this law firm if it persisted in supporting "that Jap," so Geisness was forced to leave in June 1942. Walters was a constitutional lawyer. Although he was a Republican and an American Legion member—all the qualities that normally went with being anti-Japanese—he was interested in civil liberties and felt that the incarceration was wrong. He was not a Clarence Darrow type, but he was competent and conscientious. He stayed on when the case went to the Supreme Court.

Today, September 20, 1942, I received a letter from Min Yasui. His attorney, Earl Bernard, is pessimistic about the forthcoming verdict. It seems that two of the justices were approached before the military orders were issued. Consequently, there are two sustaining votes there. And further, the fact that the decision will be the result of political philosophy rather than sociological, ethical, or legal concepts suggests more sustaining votes. Most of the justices are New Dealers, President Roosevelt's selections. It seemed the most we could hope for is a brilliant and powerful dissenting opinion of the Holmes and Cardozo type. Yasui sounded very disappointed, but he tenaciously hangs on to his optimism and to the faith that the Supreme Court will come through as it should. My attorney feels that the court has already decided the question before our cases have been heard. Things don't look too bright, legally. I may be busting rocks soon.

It is less than a week until my trial. I don't know how one is supposed to feel in such a moment, but I don't seem to feel any different. At least I don't seem to be worked up. Perhaps it is because I'm looking beyond this trial to the later appeals to the circuit court and the Supreme Court. Perhaps it is because I hold such little hope, if any, of a favorable decision. I don't think it is a feeling of defeat; it is more a feeling of awareness of the present climate and an attempt to face reality. Legal courts may throw the book at me, but a "higher court" shall see that in time justice will prevail. For such a time I live. Until such a time, may the Eternal Spirit keep me buoyed and tender in the spirit of love.

On Monday, October 13, I was due in court for the hearing on the plea for abatement. However, as District Attorney Hile was out of town, it was postponed. On Thursday morning, I was suddenly called to court. My demurrer was sternly rejected on the basis of "wartime necessity." A date for my trial was set—October 20. As this case will likely center around the question of my loyalty and character, I am preparing thoughts along those lines. Frank Walters is coming up soon to check with me about my parents' background, my own background, my connection with Japan, etc. I wonder if we will discuss curfew and evacuation in court.

The trial began on October 20, 1942, with Judge Lloyd L. Black presiding. After the jury was sworn in, I was charged with both curfew and exclusion order violations. The government prosecutor, Allen Pomeroy, called Dad up as a witness to confirm the fact that I am of Japanese ancestry. That wasn't necessary, as I was never saying anything otherwise. Dad was a bit hesitant in answering as he's not a public speaker type.

Frank Walters said, "Your Honor, I think we should get an interpreter for him."

And the judge said, "Oh, by all means. Is there anyone here in this place who could interpret for the witness?"

Nobody raised a hand—so I said, "Well, I could interpret for him, if you can accept the defendant."

They said, "Well, okay."

So I interpreted: "Where were you born? Do you have any children here, in the United States? Is anyone here in this courtroom?"

And Dad looked at me funny, saying, "Yes."

Then prosecutor Pomeroy said, "Can you point to your son?"

Dad points to me, the guy who is translating!

Frank Walters argued that the Fifth Amendment right of due process was violated by the exclusion order, emphasizing that I had never been accused of posing a danger for espionage or sabotage, the two ostensible reasons for the exclusion proclamation. Walters moved the court to dismiss the indictment on the grounds that the defendant had been deprived of liberty and property without due process of law and that Executive Order 9066, Proclamations 2 and 3, Civilian Exclusion Order 57 of the military commander, and Public Law 503 are all unconstitutional and void. The motion was denied by the trial court, to which the defendant excepted and his exception was allowed.

District Attorney Gerald Hile's arguments were few and, to my way of thinking, evaded the issues raised.

Judge Black made a few insignificant statements. He felt that the Constitution ought to be flexible enough so that America could protect itself: "We have been engaged in a total war . . . with enemies [who are] unbelievably treacherous and wholly ruthless. The due process argument should not be permitted to endanger all of the constitutional rights of the whole citizenry. Therefore we have got to take certain measures we feel are necessary for the successful prosecution of war. The military curfew and evacuation orders were reasonable protections against the diabolically clever use of infiltration tactics by potential Japanese saboteurs."

The judge gave these instructions to the jury:

You can forget all the talk about the Constitution by the defense.
What is relevant here is the public proclamation issued by the West-

ern Defense Command. You are to determine this: is the defendant a person of Japanese ancestry? If so, has he complied with the military curfew and exclusion orders, which are valid and enforceable laws? It is your duty to accept the laws as stated by the Court, despite any opinion of your own that the law should be different. . . . You are instructed to return a finding of guilty, and if you will not, you are violating your oath.

That was the conclusion of my "trial." The obedient jury was out only ten minutes before returning with a guilty verdict. The judge pronounced me guilty of each offense charged in the two counts of the indictment. My trial lasted just one day. It started in the morning, the jurors took a noon recess, and it continued in the afternoon until my conviction.

Judge Lloyd Black denied my constitutional challenge. He trotted out "Yellow Peril" stereotypes, labeling the Japanese as unbelievably treacherous and "shrewd masters of trickery and concealment among any who resemble them." In the end, Judge Black said, "Well, this is the sentencing time, and you have been charged with two counts, and I am going to take into account that the maximum for each count is twelve months. I realize that you have been waiting more than five months in jail. I am going to consider that, and in the light of that, I am going to sentence you to thirty days for the curfew violation and thirty days for the exclusion order violation, to be served consecutively for a total of sixty days. Does the prisoner have anything to say?"

In retrospect, I should have left it alone. I told my attorney to inquire if the judge could add fifteen days to each of the counts so it would be forty-five days for each, making ninety days. The reason for this seemingly odd request was that a fellow prisoner and "jailhouse lawyer" advised me that I would have to get at least ninety days if I wanted to serve my time outdoors in a road camp. Otherwise, the Bureau of Prisons would not take the trouble to move me from jail to a road camp.

The judge laughed and said, "I can accommodate, but why don't we simplify the matter by making it ninety days on each count to be served concurrently?" We all agreed to that.

THE APPEALS PROCESS

After I was sentenced, we appealed, and I continued to remain in jail because the judge and I couldn't agree on bail conditions. He said, "If your backers put up the bail, I will release you to one of the barbed wire internment camps."

I answered, "If my backers put up bail, I should be released out the front door just like anybody else."

He retorted, "There's a law that says you're not allowed out in the streets, so I can't do that."

So the motion was denied by the court. I excepted to the court's ruling, and my exception was allowed.

Returning again to prison, battered and shaken, my erstwhile grip on the Constitution as the beacon to keep the light in these dark days loosened seriously. Am I any longer able to stand unquestioningly behind the Constitution? It was not only me—there were 110,000 persons of Japanese ancestry in concentration camps solely on the basis of ancestry. What good is the Constitution if it cannot stand up in a crisis? And yet . . . there is an East African Basuto proverb that advises: "Do not abandon your old ways unless there is something of value to replace it." If I now toss out the Constitution, with what can I replace it to serve as my beacon of hope that would permit me to maintain my personal integrity, that would give me the strength to go forth with a positive perspective?

Throughout, I remained convinced that I had taken the correct stand. I fully expected that the Constitution would protect me, as a citizen. Surprisingly, even though I lost, I did not abandon my beliefs and values. It did not come as a magical flash; rather it emerged as a sort of a natural metamorphosis. There is nothing wrong with the Constitution. If it appeared good in the past, it is still potentially good. If the promised protection did not materialize, it is because those entrusted to uphold it have failed to uphold it. Ultimately, the buck stops here, with me, with us, the citizens. If we care enough and stop rationalizing, the Constitution can be meaningful. Otherwise, it can be no more than a scrap of paper on which it is printed. It is up to us.

Mary Farquharson came to discuss the possibilities of my leaving on bond pending appeal. She thinks there is a very good possibility that such an opportunity will be presented to me by the district attorney and the judge. If I can leave on bond to points east, then Mary wanted to know if I would go. I said that on principle I saw no conflict. I had previously discussed it with Floyd Schmoe. Legally, the case goes on regardless of where I am. Mary feels strongly that being out is better, as personal contacts I make will help in the case as well as arouse interest and sympathy toward all Japanese Americans. I'm beginning to feel that I can do more by being out, but when I consider the possibility of leaving, I experience conflicting emotions. To get out of this district altogether is a saddening thought. There are too many things and people that I'll miss, and some very badly. But then, how many thousands went through the same sad experience—only worse? I want to get out and I want to stay. Doggone it, why can't I get out and remain in Seattle?

SAN FRANCISCO COURT OF APPEALS

On December 9, 1942, Frank Walters wrote, "The appeal has been completed. I have filed my opening brief and expect to get the government's answering brief tomorrow. Mr. Dennis and I are going to enter into a stipulation asking that the hearing on the appeal be set for the earliest date possible, which may be later this month or in January in San Francisco. Judge Fee's decision will be of great help, even though it has been severely criticized."

Ray Roberts told me that the appeal hearing has been scheduled for January. It seems that all of the appellate judges are going to sit in, rather than the usual three or so. Honestly speaking, I do not hope for a favorable decision. But I'm hoping and hoping hard.

When the case was being transferred from the San Francisco circuit court (court of appeals) to the Supreme Court in February 1943, the federal judge in Seattle contacted my attorney and proposed: "Your boy has been confined in King County Jail for nine months. Shouldn't we get him out?"

"Well, Your Honor, he won't accept your condition of posting bond and then being released to a camp."

"But I can't accept his demand that he be released in Seattle. There must be an acceptable compromise."

There was. Eventually, we worked out an agreement where the judge would release me without restriction and on my own recognizance if I would agree to stay out of Military Area No. 1 for the duration of the case.

Ray Roberts brought in a bond release, which was already countersigned by Mary Farquharson and Ray as securities. I signed my name. Now all we needed was the judge's signature, and the judge was willing to sign anytime the army or attorney general said okay. So far the army has definitely given a negative answer. An airmail letter to Attorney General Biddle has been written in an attempt to secure from him an order to the deputy marshal to escort me out of this Defense Command area. If that fails, there's one more possibility: Attorney Walters will personally approach an army official whom he knows to see if the army will reconsider its order. The main hope lies in Biddle. Will he give the orders in spite of army sentiments? After all, I'm not in the army's custody. Yet this is a Defense Command area. Who will rule whom? Does the Department of Justice take priority, or the U.S. Army? There seems to be no justification except vindictiveness, and the usual army "toughie" attitude, for keeping me here after bond arrangements have been met. Why can't I leave as a civilian under civilian instructions?

It seems Attorney General Biddle has written a favorable letter to the local district attorney, who then gave the marshal the order to escort me out. It is as I have wished: a release on bond through the court and not through the army. The only thing I do not relish is that I must leave this area. Perhaps soon I may return or at least will be free to return.

Less than two weeks away, I'm looking forward to this hearing with great anticipation. As time goes on, my hopes rise, even in the legal sense. Although the judges on the West Coast are right in the evacuation area and may be too closely concerned to be objective about my case, there are grounds for hope, that is, Judge Fee resides in Portland. And if they ever go by the books, they can't justify this order. Regardless, we can rest assured, for we know we have already triumphed in the deeper sense. But why don't they take me down to see this? Gee, I miss everything on the outside.

One more appellant has been added to the appeal hearing coming up this February 19, 1943. Min Yasui, presently being held in Multnomah County Jail, has joined our ranks. The addition of his attorney will aid our side quite a bit, I believe. Yasui's case will bring in a new angle, as his is the only one bringing a favorable decision from the lower courts. There is a possibility that in the process of gaining his status as a citizen, he may lose the main decision handed out by Judge Fee—the ruling that the army had no authority over citizens in the absence of martial law. Yasui's attorney will concentrate on Min's citizenship but will introduce and depend on Judge Fee's decision for the other part, regarding curfew against Nisei.

By then, Fred Korematsu's case had reached the U.S. Court of Appeals. The justices met for the arguments on the three cases. In the course of their deliberations, they framed fundamental questions to the Supreme Court for guideline assistance. In essence, the Supreme Court informed the circuit court that they might as well have the cases transferred. In five weeks (March 27, 1943), the transfer to the Supreme Court was made, bypassing a circuit court decision.

Fresno Bee (November 28, 1943) letter to the editor states that native birth does not necessarily signify citizenship: "Flies, rats, snakes, pests, termites are all born here but are they citizens? And so why should the Japs be citizens merely because of birth?"

Maybe the letter writer's got something. Sometimes some of us think we are quite akin to many of the unwanted pests that populate this earth and hope that some humanitarian will painlessly exterminate us. And then, we rise to our dignity and challenge being so insulted. Thus there remains hope for progress. I am a chronic optimist. I cannot despair for long.

CHAPTER 13

U.S. Supreme Court

MARCH 27, 1943—THE COURT OF APPEALS PASSED MY CASE TO the Supreme Court to decide the constitutionality of Public Law 503 and the Western Defense commander DeWitt's curfew and evacuation orders.

We retained Harold Evans, a Quaker lawyer from Philadelphia with Supreme Court experience, who said, "There is a good bit of sympathy in Quaker circles for Hirabayashi, a high type of man." He reasonably asked for postponement to acquaint himself with the intricacies of the case and to prepare his strategy. Postponement was denied, and the hearing took place as scheduled.

I still maintain my faith in the nine old men and trust that they will do what they deem just. Even if our views differ, I shall not change in my regard for a decision handed down in sincerity.

My case was appealed to the U.S. Supreme Court on May 10, 1943, with Chief Justice Harlan Stone presiding. The outcome of the war was uncertain, and the mysterious phrase "military necessity" still carried a huge wallop. From the district court to the Supreme Court in seven months is bordering on record quickness. Normally, it takes much longer. We were anticipating about a two-year period and hoping that the hearing would occur during a time when hysteria would have waned, if not disappeared.

Congress was tired of having the Supreme Court taking certain prerogatives that were legislative by using a case, making sweeping conclusions, and springboarding into congressional prerogatives.

Congress said the Court should confine itself to the requirements of the trial. If a person were guilty of something, just sentence him to that. If a person is serving concurrent sentences, take one of the cases. Then there is no ruling on the other case because the person is automatically serving time, which covers the time to be served in both cases.

During the Court's conference, members Roberts, Reed, Douglas, Rutledge, and Murphy voiced serious doubts about the legality and constitutional basis of DeWitt's orders. In early June, Justice Frank Murphy had circulated a draft of a dissent to his fellow jurors, stating that discrimination among citizens on the basis of their ancestry was "so utterly inconsistent with our ideas and traditions, and in my judgment so contrary to constitutional requirements, that I cannot lend my assent." He was talked out of his dissent by Justice Felix Frankfurter, who asserted that any break in unanimous support for the army in wartime amounted to "playing into the hands of the enemy." Faced with this challenge to his patriotism, Murphy capitulated, changed his statement to "going to the very brink of constitutionality," and went along with the majority.

After they spent 90 percent of the time on the exclusion order, they focused on the curfew order. They went into chambers, and Chief Justice Stone said, "This case has two counts, and the sentences are concurrent. Since Hirabayashi's sentences were to run concurrently, it is unnecessary for the court to consider the questions raised by his conviction for failure to report to a civil control station. His conviction for violation of the curfew order was an obvious preliminary to his exclusion from the Pacific Coast." They took, in other words, the curfew issue and said that they didn't need to rule on the other. "The questions for the court to decide were whether the curfew order by General DeWitt was an exercise of an unconstitutional delegation by Congress of its legislative powers, and whether the order unconstitutionally discriminated against persons of Japanese ancestry in violation of the Fifth Amendment. We take one to see if the person is guilty or not."

On June 21, 1943, Chief Justice Stone upheld the curfew conviction, writing: "The danger of espionage and sabotage to our military resources was imminent and the curfew order was an appropriate measure to meet it." It permitted the court to "present a front of rather wary unanimity to the world." With characteristic flattery, Frankfurter placed his benediction on Stone's final product. "You have labored with great forbearance and with concentration to produce something worthy of the Torah."

In the checks-and-balances system of the United States, the judicial, legislative, and executive branches of the government jealously guard their respective prerogatives. But the Supreme Court seemingly abdicated its duty to defend and uphold the Constitution, deferring to the executive branch, saying, "You're the specialists running the war, and who are we to tell you what to do?" or something to that effect. Even with information classified in many respects, the justices could have sought particulars before abandoning the Constitution. Why in Hawai'i was it considered militarily feasible to investigate on an individual basis regarding national security, whereas it was "military necessity" to uproot the entire Japanese American population on the West Coast on the basis of ancestry? Particularly when you count the fact that Hawai'i had already been subject to a devastating air attack, while the West Coast had not, and the Japanese American population in Hawai'i, more than one-third of the territory's total, was more than double the number on the West Coast. The Supreme Court neglected to make this inquiry.

I thought that the raison d'être for the Supreme Court was to uphold the Constitution. I didn't realize the extent to which World War II hysteria had swept up everyone. I always felt the Supreme Court was a cut above everybody else. I think the justices are outstanding people. But in this case—if we lose the case—there is no Constitution. The country itself is a priority. The Supreme Court didn't say that; Judge Black did. He is like the attorney for the army. He felt that whatever the proclamation of the military commander, it was constitutional because it followed in direct line from Executive Order 9066, which Roosevelt as commander in chief was authorized to issue. What's the sense of defending a Constitution if we don't even have a country? So the country is the priority.

I wasn't in attendance at the trial. I was with my parents in Idaho, so I didn't go. I read about the decision in the paper. I heard a little bit about the hearing. My perspectives on the court presentations, decisions, and all that—I was relatively naive—were just a citizen's view. With many fewer civil rights cases, we just weren't familiar with the issues. I expected that when it got to the Supreme Court, of course, they were going to declare curfew and incarceration unconstitutional. President Roosevelt wanted a decision in favor of the government. He apparently passed the word to one of his appointees that it would be a good thing for the war effort if there was a unanimous decision. Justice Murphy had circulated a draft of his intention to dissent. So they worked on him, and finally, he caved in. He was persuaded to restate it as "going to the very brink of constitutionality," and he went along with the majority. Later, in his dissent in the Korematsu case, he said that "it falls into the ugly abyss of racism." Well, I thought—I guess the Constitution had gone to war, too!

Looking back on it all, in the Supreme Court decisions having to do with the basic rights of Japanese Americans during a time of war (*Hirabayashi v. United States*, in June 1943, and *Korematsu v. United States* and *Ex Parte Endo* in December 1944), the court left prominent loopholes. Its tautology can be summarized as follows:

1. Where there is a compelling social circumstance, individual rights must give way;
2. Exclusion from specified areas and detention in confined places may be necessary for military security;
3. Therefore, all persons of Japanese ancestry must be uprooted and detained in camps.

In *Ex Parte Endo*, the court ruled in favor of Endo, stating that the government did not have the right to detain a citizen without charges. Therefore, Endo must be released from camp. But the court did not raise the question of why she was in camp in the first place. That question could have been raised in *Hirabayashi* or *Korematsu*. By doing so, the court would have had an opportunity to try to explain how point 3 above would emerge from the first two premises. How does a specific action regarding the removal of a particular group on the basis of ancestry follow from the first two premises? Yet the highest court managed to defeat *Hirabayashi* 8–0 and *Korematsu*, a year and a half later, 6–3.

In his *Korematsu* dissent, Supreme Court justice Robert Jackson opined, "A military order, however unconstitutional, is not apt to last longer than the military emergency. . . . But once a judicial opinion rationalizes such an order, the court for all time has validated the principle of racial discrimination . . . ready for the hand of any authority that can bring forward a plausible claim of an urgent need."

CHAPTER 14

Out on Bail

AFTER THE TRIAL, WITH THE STALEMATE OVER MY BAIL TERMS, I remained in jail four months into the appeal period. By that time, Judge Black was willing to release me. We'd become sort of like old friends, in terms of his knowledge of me, and he said, "We ought to get him out." We worked out a compromise that I would go to Spokane, which was outside of the restricted area for Japanese Americans. Judge Black said, "I want you to promise that you will not return to the restricted area for the duration of the appeal." That sounded acceptable to me, so I went out to Spokane.

Nevin Sayre had written offering a job with the Fellowship of Reconciliation and hoped I would accept. I certainly appreciated his kindness, but right now I would prefer work with the American Friends Service Committee for various reasons. The Quakers had contacted the Philadelphia office of the AFSC, which was by that time working on resettlement of camp residents wherever they could, looking for housing and jobs. "Spokane is a part of Eastern Washington, which was not in a Defense Command area. Therefore, let's post Gordon there. We'll open up a temporary field station and let him run it and find jobs and housing. He can also do public relations to increase the public's awareness about those two items." So that's what I was released for.

By February 11, Floyd Schmoe of the AFSC verified everything concerning my release. All plans being completed, the only question was, Saturday night or Sunday night? Floyd worried about my clothes, overcoat, shirt, shoes, etc. After some consideration, we decided that it would be better to do most of the shopping in Spokane after I got out. The plan for now was that I travel east with the marshal and meet Floyd in Spokane. Then we'll travel to Heart Mountain camp, and from there to Colorado. This plan is ideal! I have been dreaming about it, never realizing it would be a reality. That is the best thing that could happen to me—the ideal setup for my adjustment to "free world" living again. I must not, in my youthful excitement, forget the kind of world I'm stepping into. I must be prepared to spend much effort in the release of evacuees from camp to outside life. I hope my hand shall be useful.

Yesterday, February 12, at 8:30 a.m., I parted with my friends at King County Jail. Harry Ault, Tacoma marshal, drove me to his office in his new Dodge. The scenery was wonderful and refreshing. The radio was simply divine; it was such a change to hear good music. At Tacoma I sat in the front office like an official all day, sending cards to my friends about the good news. My first "free world" meal since October 20 was a hamburger steak, lettuce and tomato salad, mashed potatoes with gravy, custard pie, and good coffee. It was wonderful. I was amused to find myself almost at a loss in manipulating the fork. Then Esther Schmoe and June Mott scooted up. Those two always find me. I don't believe I can ever get lost as long as those two are on my trail.

The marshal and I took the day coach to Seattle and then switched to our Pullman car, which finally pulled out around 9:45 p.m. and arrived in Spokane in the morning. We got one of those end compartments with a double bunk. So I was on the upper bunk, and the marshal took the lower bunk. I wasn't excited, but I was leaving after nine months. I hadn't considered it seriously till I was moving out because I've sort of settled into thinking that I'm going to sit it out here for the duration. Of course, nobody knew what "duration" meant either. I talked with the marshal most of the trip about all sorts of things, sports to politics for half of the night, and then dozed off.

On the morning of February 15, I met Floyd Schmoe. He asked, "How was the train ride?" I said it was fine although a little crowded. I described the setup. He said, "I wish we had known about it. We would have protested. We bought that cabin, the end compartment." That evening, we attended an informal meeting of the Spokane FOR group. This was the first home that I had stepped into since last May, and I really enjoyed it. We had a very fine meeting.

I got a room at the YMCA. I stayed there until summer. The work program that was approved with the federal office, the court office, was that I would be working with the American Friends Service Committee on the resettlement process of people moving from camps back to regular life. Spokane was one of the places for those settling in Eastern Washington as well as those people who preferred locating in Spokane, rather than moving to the Midwest or back East, until such time as Seattle became available for a move. So those who wished for a western return found Spokane a viable option.

Floyd and I were trying to crash the Issei society in camp (with the help of an interpreter). An adult education director planned on several meetings this week. One of the heaviest factors against resettlement generally came from the Issei, who were leery of anything advocated by the WRA or army. When WRA and army officials talked up resettlement, the general Issei attitude was, "So they want to toss us out now, eh? Well, we want to stay." Talks with several Issei convinced me that a volunteer outsider such as Floyd would swing the Issei onto the right track. They appreciated Floyd's sincerity and tended to cooperate. This, I felt, would be an important venture.

When we were looking for employment for people, a laundry business was one of the places that had advertised, and so we called them about openings. I told Esther, "Why don't you go in?" and I waited in the car. She came out about fifteen minutes later looking flustered and upset. She got into the car and broke down and wept for five minutes. It turned out that the conversation went fine; jobs were confirmed as they needed people badly. But when they discovered that the candidates were of Japanese ancestry, the owners said, "Hell no! We can't. We don't want to take a chance hiring Japanese." She argued about it with them, and it was a stone wall. This was the first time—Esther was about twenty—the first time she'd run into this kind of frontal objection. It was a real shock to her. However, it made me realize how I had compartmentalized these things without letting it affect my pride in being an American. It didn't seem to affect me in that way, since I could push it aside and rationalize it. This wasn't the only occasion when we had problems dealing with resettlement.

Dr. Paul Suzuki was a prominent Issei doctor in Seattle before the war. His wife, Nobu, a Nisei, was on the University YWCA board. During the latter part of July 1943, Nobu Suzuki left Minidoka in Idaho for Spokane in search of a livable house. Like other cities, Spokane is suffering from an acute housing shortage; therefore, renting or leasing was out of the question. There were, however, a few houses for sale, which Nobu considered.

A large, six-room, well-built brick house with a spacious lawn and well-kept shrubbery appealed to her very much. This house was for sale at $6,000 and required a $2,000 down payment. Although this house was not located in the best district, it was in about the best district now available to the Japanese.

Arrangement for purchase was made with Mrs. Klein, the seller, and Arthur D. Jones Real Estate, the agents. Upon advice from her attorney, Mrs. Klein changed her terms of cash to $5,900, probably due to the fact that the purchasers were of Japanese descent. This called for some maneuvering on the part of Mrs. Suzuki. She approached several banks for loans. She was turned down in every attempt because Dr. Suzuki had been born in Japan and because of the community property laws in this state. It is true that Mrs. Suzuki is an American-born citizen, but it is also true that the banks are rather conservative. In a final attempt, she called her brother, Mako Yanagimachi, who was living in Caldwell, Idaho, to help her make the purchase. Mako Yanagimachi is an American citizen, as is his wife. Mako came to Spokane immediately and satisfactorily made arrangements for the purchase of the house. The house where the Suzukis now live, 1626 E. Pacific Avenue, belongs to Makoto Yanagimachi. The Suzukis will take out the papers to lease the house from Mrs. Suzuki's brother. Mrs. Suzuki stayed in Spokane three weeks to complete the purchase of the house and thereby assured herself and her family of a home in Spokane. It was with great joy and satisfaction that she returned to Minidoka in the middle of August to pack up for her first step in resettlement.

Until the Suzukis moved in, I had agreed to take care of their lawn. On Saturday, August 21, I was mowing the lawn. A car stopped, and a man got out and approached me. "Japs purchased this place? Well, they can't move in. My name's Burke, and I represent the Union Park District, and we don't want Japs moving in. If they want to stay healthy, they'd better not move in." The fact that the purchasers were citizens and that the wife was a citizen made no difference. "As far as I'm concerned, you're just Japs to us." The fact that Union Park was a mediocre district and definitely not an "exclusive" district was overlooked (or ignored). A petition was circulated to oust the Suzukis; this information came from one of the neighbors who refused to sign. Mrs. Suzuki said it would take a lot to move her out.

During the week, Mrs. Klein and the Arthur D. Jones Real Estate Company were approached several times with threats of legal action and violence, if necessary, to the property. Both, particularly Mr. Jones, were getting alarmed and thinking it wiser to acquiesce to neighbors' demands.

While watering the lawn, I was handed a letter by S. J. Burke. The letter was addressed to the purchasers and occupants of the house at 1626 E. Pacific Avenue and to the Arthur D. Jones company. It was written by attorney Lester Edge, a member of one of the leading law firms in Spokane. The essence of the letter was that since Dr. Suzuki is an alien, and since the house was bought by a citizen for him, it may be escheated to the state of Washington. In addition, the neighbors did not want them, so it would be wisest not to take occupancy and to sell the property. The situation could no longer be shrugged off. It was now approaching a stage where some precautions had to be taken, particularly against violence of some sort.

On September 14, somebody drove by and tossed a large rock through the front living room window. I wasn't there at the time, but I was pleased that Nobu Suzuki took a very philosophical view of it. Instead of raising all sorts of high-tension responses, she took it in stride and said, "I'm going to make use of that rock, because this is good as a weight for my barrel, where I make pickles."

The vandalism at the Suzuki home, along with threats by Burke and company, resulted in radio and newspaper notices. The Suzukis were ably supported by many friends. Things cooled down a bit, but the protests were apparently not finished yet. In response to this unfortunate situation, the Spokane Fellowship of Reconciliation really took hold, the Ernsts in particular.

Myron Ernst went to the chief of police, who had no suggestions. Myron felt that there was little hope of action from the police. This may have been just as well. I felt, and told them, that in the growing group of friendly neighbors, the Suzukis have their best protection. I advised Myron to talk to the prosecuting attorney himself but to take legal action only as a last resort. I felt that once the "gang" knows that the better element in the neighborhood is actively friendly, they would hesitate to press the case.

I thought it might even be a good thing in the end, as Paul Suzuki would need to make acquaintances in order to start a practice. This way he was making contacts fast, and the majority of them were sympathetic. He did not attempt to find office space yet and may delay it, doing odd jobs around the hospital for a time. The staff and doctors attached to the Deaconess Hospital were all, or nearly all, cooperative. Dr. Suzuki had fewer contacts at the Catholic Hospital (St. Joseph's, I believe, and the only other large hospital in town), but those he had were friendly. There were several Nisei nurses and students at the Deaconess.

Just at this time, Floyd Schmoe and family came to Spokane. He couldn't have timed his visit better; as he said, "I wired Reverend William Gold to get his friendly people together and call on Burke. I also advised him to consult with Ben Kiser (American Civil Liberties Union attorney) the prosecuting attorney, as well as the police." Floyd also made a long-distance call to Seattle to Mary Farquharson, former state senator and Pacific Northwest secretary of the FOR, who has Spokane contacts and knows attorney Lester Edge personally.

Mary Farquharson called Kiser, who said that Mrs. Suzuki had talked with him and that he had advised her to see the prosecuting attorney. A meeting was called that evening at the home of the Suzukis. Rev. Bill Gold, Lela Wogman, Myron and Helen Ernst of the FOR, Theodora Crane and Joe Wilkening of the Friends, the Schmoes, and I were present. The fact that the opposing attorney was a member of the leading law firm in town demanded serious thinking on our part. Was that letter a threat, or a bluff? There was research to be done.

During the following three days, Mary and Floyd covered the town. Mary used her key contacts to advantage. It helped very much that she knew attorney Edge. Mr. Ben Kiser of the ACLU and Fair Play Committee came to our aid. Mr. Kiser is an outstanding lawyer in town. Mr. Jones of the real estate company was visited and "bolstered" as he was getting a little weak-kneed. It was soon definitely established that there were no legal grounds for any sort of lawsuit. The threatening letter was admittedly a bluff. But there still remained another obstacle: the possibility of violence to property or person or both.

In an attempt to improve relations and create understanding rather than resort to legal opposition, all the ministers and priests in the district were contacted. Theodora Crane (Quaker) met and talked with Mr. Burke, the opposing spokesman. He appeared very agreeable. Mrs. Klein aided by securing fourteen names of residents of the district who did not object to Japanese moving in.

At about 7:30 in the evening, Mr. Burke, Mr. Finch (feed store man), and Mr. Johnson (tavern keeper), with the Sprague Street "gang"— mostly hangers-on at Johnson's tavern and mostly drunk—called on the Suzukis. They found a house full of friendly neighbors. The group included a half-dozen ministers; Monsignor Peters, the old priest of St. Ann's Church nearby; a half-dozen of his parishioners; the Ernsts; and others of the FOR.

The callers stated that they had not come to listen, only to tell the "Japs," the Suzukis, that they must move out. Mr. Finch, however, did stay and talked for two hours. He finally apologized for the drunken gang who had come along "just in case there was a fight." He said that they had nothing to do with the rock through the window and that they did not contemplate violence. He did say, however, "If we cannot oust them by legal proceedings, we will find some other way." He did not seem to know what "other way" might be found.

The Suzukis have been living at their new home without incident. The shops in the neighborhood have been very cordial to them. When Mrs. Suzuki took her son, Yosh, age six, to Edison School, everyone was friendly. Members of the FOR have called on them and invited the Suzukis to their homes. The Suzukis took out lease papers to lease the house from her brother. Mr. Kiser will handle the legal details.

CHAPTER 15

Thumbing to Jail

TOWARD THE END OF SUMMER 1943, ABOUT THREE MONTHS after the U.S. Supreme Court decision, I was in Spokane doing my work with the American Friends Service Committee. I was out on bail at the time but still faced a ninety-day sentence. One afternoon as I was mowing the lawn, a couple of guys walked up, identified themselves as FBI agents, and asked where Gordon Hirabayashi would be. I said, "I am he."

They said, "Well, we're supposed to bring you in."

I told them I was expecting them. "What took you so long?"

District Attorney Connelly said, "It's time to serve your sentence. You've got ninety days, so you can do it at the federal tank of the Spokane County Jail."

I protested, "It cost me dearly to have the sentence increased in order to serve it in a road camp, and it's unfair that I be sent back to jail."

He said, "You're not allowed to go to Military Area No. 1, and the only other one in the west is near Tucson. That's 1,600 miles away, and I don't have travel funds."

I argued that I had purposefully asked for an additional thirty days on my sentence because I wanted to be in a prison camp so that I could do outdoor work.

Although sympathetic to my plea, he replied, "Too bad. I can't help you."

Impulsively, I asked if he would approve my going to Tucson if I went on my own. He not only would approve but said, "I will write a

'To Whom It May Concern' letter to describe what you are doing so that they know you're not just roaming around illegally."

I told him I appreciated that and picked it up the next day.

I didn't want to pay my way to prison, so I guessed I'd have to hitchhike. Who in the heck would have the stupidity to hitchhike on an intermountain road during a period when there was gas rationing? It took me two weeks.

From Spokane, down through Pendleton, down to Boise, to Salt Lake, Las Vegas, Phoenix, to Tucson—that was the route I took. Near Umatilla, Oregon, there was a friendly half-moon giving me light and warmth. By 10 p.m., cars were coming every thirty minutes or so. I stood hoping until nearly midnight, then decided to call it a day. A little exploring, and I soon found a very shallow ditch, grooved, well padded with grass, and I slid down to spend the night. It was quite comfortable, and I must have dozed off for a couple hours. I awoke with my knees icy and teeth chattering. A neighbor dog was barking his head off. I lay quietly, but I guess the pooch smelled me and didn't like the whiff. Disgustedly, I grabbed my suitcase and climbed out of the ditch. There was a gently invigorating if not freezing breeze coming from the south. I sat on the baggage, waiting.

In a position and circumstance like that, a fellow has a chance to do a lot of meditating and reflecting. Things that are ordinarily overlooked are viewed in the proper perspective. Frogs sounded friendly and happy. Flickering lights in the distance seemed to be giving me a come-hither wink. Even the stars that I have seen for years had a fresh appearance. They seemed beyond approach and yet within comprehension. They seemed to be viewing the feverish ways of man, saying, "When will he ever learn?" I looked up and talked to the brightest star near the Dipper: "Dear star, will you always keep me close to the real values of life? Keep me strong so that I may live in spite of contemporary lack of understanding? Bring me the charm that will bring understanding to others, the understanding of the beauties and fullness of real living?" I guess it was 2:30 a.m. or maybe 3:00, perhaps the darkest moments of the night. From then on, things would loosen up and dawn would come. As the forerunner to dawn, a big diesel freight truck came roaring around the corner. He stopped and took me to Pendleton.

Getting out at Pendleton, I was standing in front of a gas station. I aired my thumb as occasional cars sped by. Finally a car stopped for gas and oil. Started a conversation with the driver and won a lift. He was going to call it a day at La Grande. Slowly, methodically, I convinced him that he should hit Idaho by the end of that day. Mile after mile rolled by before he finally decided to go on to Idaho. I was happy.

It took about two or three days to get to Weiser, Idaho, where I visited a few days with my parents. Early morning, Mom woke me and said she was on her way to work. Sleepily I said good-bye and that all would be well. She said she doesn't feel badly at all for my going to prison, but she choked a little. The reason was that she now knows I can handle the situation adequately and will return a stronger person. Mother made me some Japanese food: sushi, teriyaki, and rice balls. I like those better than sandwiches. They're easier to carry, tastier, and sustain me better. Hooray—a ride all the way into Salt Lake City in a '41 Packard. One flat on the way, but otherwise swell. Ham sandwich and coffee on him; he wouldn't let me treat.

Salt Lake City has turned out to be a really worthwhile visit in spite of the authorities and their "no stopover" orders. I spent a day at the wartime headquarters of the *Pacific Citizen*, the newspaper of the Japanese American Citizens League. It was a good move to drop in on Larry Tajiri, the editor. He and his wife were happy to see me. They invited me to a meeting of the Southern California ACLU and the JACL. Lawyer A. L. Wirin of the ACLU is an interesting person and a good civil liberties man. The main reason he was in town was to instigate a couple of test cases having to do with detention in War Relocation Authority centers and the right of Japanese Americans to return to the West Coast. In the first case, Wirin would like to have up to a dozen good persons to make this request and include all the names in one big case. He asked for my cooperation. I said I would have to think it over and also would like to consult my defense committee about it. I am interested very much in a test of this kind, but I sort of hesitate to become involved in a big legal case with a dozen other names. The case may involve methods and techniques not in line with my principles, and, in consideration of the others involved, I would be helpless to do anything about it. I want to be sure everything would be all right.

The other case was to combat the Supreme Court and other court rulings on evacuation. The procedure they have planned involves writing a letter to Lieutenant General Delos Emmons requesting permission to enter the restricted area, now that military necessity doesn't seem pertinent. When this request is refused, a suit would be filed on that, and court action will take place on the question of returning to the coast.

A unique day on the road. I got to a little burg called Mona in northern Utah. I was thinking I'd be stalled there 'til kingdom come. I tried every single vehicle that rolled along. One car turned around and came back. The driver asked if I were Japanese. I said, "Nope, American of Japanese ancestry." He said he just wanted to know and turned around and left. Another car backed up and the two occupants started to give me the third degree. It was the law. He asked for travel permits. I said I didn't need any, but I had one. Why? I'm a citizen— only aliens are required to have permits. I showed him my letter from the Spokane DA's office. "Hop in," the policeman who was driving said. "I'll take you as far as Cedar City. Rides are getting worse, and sentiments 'worser.'"

In central Utah, I was given another ride, this time by a sheriff. When he asked how far I was going, I replied that I was headed for the Tucson prison camp to serve a sentence. The sheriff bolted upright, nearly drove us off the road, and skidded the car to a stop. As the dust and gravel settled, I quickly told him not to worry because I have a letter authorizing the trip and showed it to him. Although somewhat puzzled by my unusual mode of travel to prison, he finally decided to keep on going without taking me into custody and take me as far as he was going.

On a lonely road in southern Utah, a farmer in a truck picked me up. He said, "You're a Chinese aren't you?"

I said, "No, I'm an American."

"I knew that," replied the farmer, "but you are a Chinese American, aren't you?"

I answered, "My parents came from Japan; therefore, I'm an American of Japanese ancestry."

After a few moments, he said, "If I had known that, I wouldn't have picked you up."

Trying to be a good Quaker, I said, "Well, I don't want to get a ride under false pretenses, so if you'll stop the truck, I'll get out."

He thought that over and said, "Well, I picked you up, so you can stay."

With time on hand, I explained to him why I was hitchhiking to prison to serve time for a wrong constitutional decision. When we reached his house, he made me go upstairs to take a bath, fed me dinner, put me back in the truck, and drove me to a well-traveled crossroad. A minor victory, but a moral one!

CHAPTER 16

Catalina Federal Honor Camp

WHEN I REPORTED TO THE U.S. MARSHAL'S OFFICE IN TUCSON, he said, "What can I do for you?"

I said, "Well, I'm supposed to report to you to serve my sentence at a road camp near here."

And he shuffled through the files and said, "What's your name? We don't have any orders to put you in, so you might as well go home."

I said, "It took me a couple of weeks to get down here, and I'd go home, but you'd probably find those papers and I would have to do this all over again." I suggested that he telephone or telegraph the U.S. attorney in Spokane, the federal judge in Seattle, and the Federal Bureau of Prisons in Washington, D.C., to clarify my status.

He said, "OK, we'll check up on this. Why don't you go out to a movie or something—they're air-conditioned—and come back about seven?" So I went to a movie, a restaurant, and then back to the marshal's office.

"We got confirmation from three places, and we also found your papers."

They drove me out that night about thirty miles north to the Federal Honor Camp, a minimum-security facility in the Santa Catalina Mountains. This place used to be a Civilian Conservation Corps camp. There are approximately two hundred inmates, and most are engaged in constructing a road to the mountain resort at the top of the hill. I joined the road crew that worked crushing and shoveling rocks into a dump truck, which was quite monotonous and a non-incentive activity, I assure you.

Consequently, by November 1943, at my request, I was transferred to the baking department. There I became "adept" at mixing, rolling, and baking bread, learning the techniques for various rolls, pies, cakes, etc. I hope to learn something by the time I leave. The next time I'm apprehended, it will probably be McNeil Island Federal Prison, and I'll join the baking crew from the beginning. It is practical—I can use it at home or for group dinners and conferences, for relief and reconstruction purposes, to mention just a few advantages.

After I washed up Sunday morning, a friendly fellow asked where from and what for. Then another asked for my name. "So you're Gordon Hirabayashi!" We had a lot in common though we had never before met and became fast friends. Before the day was over, I met five more of his pals, now my pals, too. My number is 3751.

The quarantine here is very mild and informal. We are in regular barracks and intermingle quite freely. There is a library and recreation room. The librarian and editor of the *Road Runner* had followed my Supreme Court case, and we have become good friends. The officers were very kind. The superintendent has given me a special invitation for an interview in case of any misunderstanding with the boys on racial grounds. I anticipate no trouble; in fact, we all get along very well.

After quarantine, we were placed into three different barracks: one all white, one colored (Negroes, Mexicans, and Indians), one Mexican border jumpers. By logic, I should be in the colored. White! I did not protest because it meant progress. It meant a wedge, meant an opportunity to establish better relationships among the people of different color. I was not aware of it at the moment—but all conscientious objectors of the Fellowship of Reconciliation type were closely watching where I would be placed. If I went to the colored barracks, they would have made a mature protest, and if unheeded, they would have rolled up their blankets and moved in with me. The boys admitted that if they were consistent, they would take action with Negroes and others. I guess there is much more motivation for sympathetic action toward friends.

Every one of these boys protested segregation as a general policy, and some requested transfer to the colored barracks. For my part, I registered my protest from an entirely different angle. I approached it from an inquisition attitude: Why was I placed in the white barracks, when Spanish-looking Mexicans were placed in the colored barracks? What is your basis for barracks segregation?

Vague answers followed, of course. It seemed that Japanese were always placed in the white barracks. No logic. It was explained at great length that segregation was very minor here. The men could eat together, work together, play together, visit each others' barracks. They were separated only at sleeping time. "Actually we don't have much segregation here."

I agreed and commended the improved situation. I added, if we do not segregate on all the other points with satisfying results, why do we separate at night? Why segregate at all?

Again, divorced from logic, they weakly noted that it was always done this way.

It was the opinion of conscientious objectors that relationships and treatment of peoples of different races at this facility were as favorable as could be expected, that they were far superior to other institutions. So, not being satisfied with matters as they were, but feeling that a strike or other strong measures were not in order (would probably have negative results), we decided to write letters to the Bureau of Prisons in sympathy with the striking COs back East.

There were a lot of Mexican border jumpers (those they called the "wetbacks," the ones who illegally crossed the Rio Grande River), quite a few selective service cases, many Jehovah's Witnesses, several pacifists of the FOR type. The latter group was the most aesthetic in appreciation, and I joined them once in climbing a little hill back of the camp to gaze at the beautiful, indescribable Arizona sunsets. The Native Indians were of two types. One type, which included many traditional Hopis, was objecting to being drafted into a white man's war. Then there were those who were caught selling liquor to fellow Indians or caught with liquor. And this was apparently a kind of racket, as people would plant things to get rewards for fingering people. Then there were regular prisoners: kidnappers, murderers, thieves, etc. So we had a few categories that we don't normally have in peacetime, plus the regular peacetime prisoners.

The Hopi Indians were from the old Oraibi Reservation. That is near Grand Canyon, and their history goes back to 1100 AD. I've been studying their background a little and find it extremely interesting. For one thing, I've found that, like most groups, they have a split that divides the modern from the traditionalists. I prefer the traditionalists. I feel they have the most to offer. (Just like I prefer the original Quaker principles and techniques to the usual contemporary ones. Can you feature George Fox administering Civilian Public Service under conscription?) There are (similarly) many traditional Hopis who are Quaker-like in their peace principles and are paying for it.

Hopis look like us, so they were stopped many times on suspicion that they were Japanese! They took me in because they considered me a non–pale face: "You are a brother. Our symbol is the sun; your ancestors have the Japanese flag with the sun."

There's some connection. We frequently think of ourselves as the lost tribe of Israel, and we must have had some of our people drop off in Japan on our way over here. See, we're brothers! I had very good friendships with them. They were in jail because they refused to join the army: "Why should we fight for a country that took away our land and put us in reservations? We're not going to fight for that system."

They have built holes and huts on the hillsides surrounding our camp. On the third day I was there, they said, "We'd like you to come up, and we'll give you a Native bath, a steam bath." They built a fire around stones and then poured water over the hot stones to make steam. And with the weed soap they had made, they washed my hair. Then they talked about things, as it was a kind of retreat for them, a kind of sacred place. They were sharing with me, giving me fellowship! I'll leave camp soon, a clean boy. In spite of many shortcomings here and the joy of freedom again, I'm going to miss a lot of things when I leave.

There are about a dozen Fellowship of Reconciliation members. Most of these fellows are Civilian Public Service camp walkouts or men who refused to accept 4-E. The rest were classified 1-A. There are nearly ten other conscientious objectors—Pentecostal, Mennonites, Independents, etc.—who are nearly entirely misclassification cases. Two Mennonites and two Pentecostals who were classed as 1-A now refuse to accept parole to CPS! After sitting in jail for several months, they have come to view CPS as a function of the thing they were objecting to. The thing that impressed me most about Mennonites, judging from these two fellows, is that they do very little thinking for themselves. They accept church doctrine and stand without question. As individuals, they are wonderful boys; as Mennonites, they become hard-shelled and dogmatic. To a noticeable degree I have observed such trends among Quakers, too. I think it is a dangerous sign of decay. Our society is rapidly taking the form of the rest of the sluggish churches, seeking respectability, preservation of the status quo, popularity, and conformity.

They made me the recreation director. During the day, I went around fixing up the fields. It got so boring that I requested a transfer to the baking crew. They had a chef from one of the Indian schools. The bread, pastries, desserts were terrific. So I asked if I could bake, and the last two months I was part of the baking crew.

A group of us retreat to our favorite meditation spot for a refreshing, stimulating period of quiet. My thoughts: There is no excuse for tolerating injustice or violation of the brotherhood of man merely because we are incarcerated. There is just as much need to overcome the philosophy of force here as anywhere else. And there is the equal or better-than-equal opportunity to challenge such philosophies. Here, while incarcerated, we must build within that which will carry us through crises. A period of realistic living, if there is a concern within us, can be acted upon now. Advantages of background (money, race, etc.) should not be used. That is power politics. Nor should we employ fear to gain our ends, for that is an artificial good. It must spring from understanding and justice, trust, and, more inclusively, love—the sincere desire of all concerned to live creatively. When made aware of a concern, a protest is in order; but it should not antagonize or raise barriers. If in the protest, suffering is inevitable, it should be upon the self, not upon others. Simultaneously, there should be positive action to ease the root of our concern.

Periods of meditation are Quaker in style and spirit. Under the open sky and hills, we feel very close to the nature of things. Life becomes meaningful in a vivid way. Reading the Reverend Harry Fosdick on Jesus: "Every situation He faced He judged by what the situation did to persons . . . with consciousness of His own life and power over it, possessing capacities of intellect, purposefulness, and good will, with possibilities of development inherent in Him, nowhere else existent within our ken—such is personality." This is the very stuff of life, the innermost test of our right to be alive at all. We can handle trouble constructively. I get a lot of inspiration to live.

This is a poem born here in confinement. Perhaps it is the circumstances, but I really enjoyed the beauty and purity of these few lines. It is so filling of life's deeper ways.

WHEN LOVE IS DEAD

When heaven's dome no more is blue
Or wildest wastelands bear no flowers,
When grasses cease to shine with dew
Or cardinals call from verdant bowers,
When stars fade out and sunsets red,
Then I'll believe God's love is dead.

When mother love grows cold and chill
Or marriage ripens not with age,
When great composers' pens are still
Or truth no martyr can engage,
When human tears no more are shed,
Then I'll believe man's love is dead.

Show me ideals gained by hate,
Man's noblest dreams by Malice won.

Prove that injustice aids the state,
Or peace is purchased with a gun.
When I'm convinced love's power is weak,
Some other way of life I'll seek.

I am beginning to do some reading. Have completed *Main Street, Wisdom of the Chinese*, and the latest issues of the *Christian Century*. I am looking forward to Lloyd Douglas's *The Robe*, Lin Yutang's *Days of Our Years* and *Between Tears and Laughter*.

For a good Asian point of view on the "white man's world," take Lin Yutang's latest, *Between Tears and Laughter*. He feels that the Western idea of equal distribution of canned goods isn't going to bring peace.

What is more important than the shape and configuration of the peace after the war is our method of arriving at it and our conception of the peace process. Our conception of the peace process is a mathematical one, and the Asiatic contribution to the ideas for creating peace is first of all a challenge to the adequacy of the mathematical approach. Mathematics is cold, but life is warm; that is why mathematics must always fail to explain life. Since peace is part of life, the mathematics approach must also fail to explain peace or understand peace, or create it.

Lin Yutang is not a pacifist, but I find many places where we stand on common ground.

Have been getting a lot out of Rev. Harry Fosdick's "As I See Religion." What a potent message, religion as an individual, psychological experience. "Vital religion, like good music, needs not defense but rendition." I am in complete agreement when he says that our greatest hours are never associated with the things that we master, but rather the things that master us. "The genius of Christianity lies in reverence for personality."

When I was leaving, I said to the superintendent, "I'm sure hoping this war will finish."

He said, "You want this war to finish? How about me? I want this war to finish so I can get rid of you guys. I had all these problems of objections to discrimination and objections to this procedure by you 'conshees' (COs). I want this war to end so I can settle down to the good old murderers and kidnappers who make model prisoners because they are just doing their time. They're not trying to change the system."

Three COs began a noncooperative action. They refused to work and, in various other ways, refused to cooperate with prison regulations as an all-out absolutist CO position. They feel prison cooperates with the Social Security Act by accepting COs, just as the CO camps cooperate with it. I did not entirely agree with this point of view. Just before leaving, I was asked by a CO to carry out a note complaining about the treatment at the federal facility. I was dismayed because he came at the last minute and thus I couldn't sew it into my clothing. I would risk discovery by attempting to smuggle this sheet out. I felt no obligation to obey all the prison rules and felt this message of sufficient importance to risk taking a chance. These boys took their stand, and I wanted them to have as fair a hearing as possible.

When I left the jail, a sheet presenting the noncooperative COs' points of view was plastered onto the sole of my left foot. Upon discovery, a misconduct report was filed against me. I answered accusations of underhandedness by replying that I could justify my action in my own mind but not in theirs. It is entirely within my sense of integrity as long as I am not asked to make false statements. I took this risk knowing that discovery would bring on some punishment. As long as I feel the punishment is not too extreme or beyond call, I will accept it. Wotta life!

Wonder what's in store for me? This is an adequate finishing touch to the curfew-evacuation noncooperator and his three months' confinement. Court action, found guilty. My penalty was the loss of one day of December camp time, plus a recommendation to the director that I should forfeit my previous good time of eight days. I spent the extra time in the Pima County Jail. I'll be out on December 15. My warning to everyone is, don't get incarcerated in Pima. It's the worst jail I've ever been in.

In this Pima County Jail tank, I am renewing acquaintanceship with some old friends, Joe Cockroach and his family. Or rather, should I say, Joe's cousin La Cucaracha and his merry family. Joe probably would feel highly insulted about my referring to La Cucaracha as his cousin, but they have identically shaped bodies and the same number of legs. I know that Joe will claim differences. His family up north is much lighter, and the type of garbage they raid is much more dignified than what La Cucaracha goes after. The cockroaches in whatever section of the country add atmosphere to the county jails and make me feel at home.

I'll be leaving soon. The date will be December 7—what an irony! It was events following that day that led to my life of incarceration. For the second straight year, I'm celebrating "Pearl Harbor Day" in an appropriate manner, penned behind bars like a dangerous animal. I wish I were a dangerous animal. Then I might feel justified being here.

I merely rewrote the letter they confiscated and sent it on after I got out of the Pima jail. I began my jail career with a nine-month sojourn. This was followed by a three-month federal sentence. Will it be done for good with this nine-day cell? Isn't it sort of poetic, beginning and ending with nine?

After I left, I discovered that Tucson was also in Military Area Zone A, restricted for everyone of Japanese ancestry. The reason I was in Tucson was because I wasn't allowed to go to McNeil Island Penitentiary due to the restriction. Unknown to myself and the federal government, I was sent to a forbidden area. Had I known, I could have enjoyed that thrill of putting one over on them!

My ticket to Spokane states "By government request and no stopovers." I am to report to the district attorney upon my arrival. I will entirely ignore the letter. I will see the DA and be on friendly terms if possible, but I will drop in casually at a later date in order to see my old friend Max Etter, assistant DA. Reporting to the DA is not a custom required of ordinary released prisoners. It was asked of me because of my ancestry. I shall consider it, therefore, in the same light as I consider evacuation.

CHAPTER 17

Federal Prison Again

FEBRUARY 1944—THERE WERE A NUMBER OF EFFORTS OF THE leaders of the Japanese American Citizens League to get the government to restore normal citizenship rights to the Japanese Americans. My position on the camps, to the extent it was known to the Japanese community, was an embarrassment to them. I never got support from them; I never asked for it. The Nisei leaders of the JACL, in order to cooperate with the government, made an early move to reopen the Selective Service System for the Nisei who had been classified as "enemy aliens" so that they could prove their loyalty to America.

My cousin Joe Hirabayashi told me that a postman stopped him in downtown Spokane and asked if he knew me. He told the postman he would deliver my mail. It was the questionnaire for citizens of Japanese ancestry from the Seattle Draft Board. Should I fill it in and return it, return it unfilled-in with a letter attached, or ignore the questionnaire? Eighty percent of the items were redundant; they were on the regular questionnaire that I had already filled in. The rest of it had to do with various kinds of questions dealing with loyalty, because of Japanese ancestry, including questions 27: Are you loyal to the emperor of Japan? and 28: Are you willing to serve in the U.S. military? These two questions created the "yes-yes" / "no-no" issue and the resulting "no-no boys," the Nisei who answered in the negative as long as the Japanese Americans were incarcerated in concentration camps.

I had to go to great lengths arguing with my local draft board that my position was a positive one, that of desiring to be a conscientious citizen. It was this desire that for me prevented participation in the military as a way of achieving peace and democracy and other ideals for which we stood. I sent a letter to the draft board. "Did you check the files to see if my records are in there? If they are, do you want me to fill this in again, or is that good enough? Secondly, did you send this loyalty questionnaire as standard stuff to all persons, or only to persons of Japanese ancestry?" And I never heard anything for three weeks, so I sent back a cover letter without filling in the questionnaire. "I presume you only send these to Japanese . . . I can't participate in a policy based on racial discrimination." After about six weeks, the FBI came and said, "We're supposed to pick you up." So I was checked into jail.

I had a disappointing interview with Erickson, the assistant DA. He advised me to fill in the questionnaire. I began to get chatty and told him why I felt it was impossible for me to do so. He said he personally agreed with me, but this was war and we had to win it. "If the War Department issued this to Japanese, they must have a good reason."

Spokane Chronicle, February 15, 1944:

> Gordon Kiyoshi Hirabayashi, 25-year-old Japanese-American who previously lost a court challenge of the army's right to evacuate him from the west coast, informed United States Attorney J. Charles Dennis yesterday he is refusing to fill out a draft board questionnaire because it involves "racial discrimination."

And the headline from the *Seattle Post-Intelligencer*: "Seattle Jap Defies U.S." The story implies that I wished to withhold certain information concerning investments in Japan and registration of citizenship with Japan.

After a month or so, I was ordered to go to a Civilian Public Service camp, a camp for conscientious objectors, in eastern Oregon. This was like going to a camp, a military induction; so when the order came, I knew I wasn't going to accept it. So I just ignored it. I was told that when the train got to the camp and I wasn't on it, all of the COs cheered as there were a lot of frustrated people in camp and some of them subsequently left.

In about six weeks, the FBI came for me. "We're supposed to pick you up." I was checked into jail, but Ray Roberts, the treasurer of my defense committee, bailed me out. At that time, I was still working for the American Friends Service Committee, helping to resettle people from camp.

December 5, 1944:

REPORT OF DISPOSITION OF CRIMINAL CASE
(DEPT. CIRCULAR NO. 3429)

On November 30, 1944, the above case was disposed of as to the defendant Gordon K. Hirabayashi charged with violating Section 311, title 50, U.S.C.A. statute.

The court trial was set with Louis B. Schwellenburg, the judge who was also a former senator. I told Schwellenburg that I was handling my own case.

He said, "I kind of hesitate to let you go on, but I'm going to do it under the condition that if I find that you need a lawyer, I'm going to stop this trial and appoint a lawyer." During the trial, he was practically interfering. "Now you do this . . ." He was like my advisor—an unwanted advisor!

I made a plea of nolo contendere. I explained my conscientious objection stance. It was my belief, and I wasn't using the Quaker name. Ray Roberts testified. He drew a laugh when he reminded the judge, "I used to support you in your campaigns . . ." Ray provided some background as to my activities relating to pacifism when I was a student at the University of Washington.

The judge said, "I'm taking into consideration that Gordon has certain religious principles; however, in terms of a decision, the jury's decision is final. In view of the fact that he has these scruples, I am going to sentence him to twelve months. Also, every month you work at McNeil Island camp, you get three days off." With statutory good time off, it was ten months.

Seattle Times, December 28, 1944:

When I was sentenced in Spokane, I left with a group of twenty men headed for McNeil. When we got there, they stripped us and handed us prison jeans and lined us up alphabetically and issued numbers in sequence. I was number 1400. We were put into the "fish tank," kept there for thirty days, and then transferred to one of the dorms. There were three main dormitories on the farm. One of them was where they put all the non-whites, and the other two dorms were for whites.

At the end of the month, I heard my name called by the night officer. "Your name was called. You and three others."

I went over to pick up my gear, and here's this guy, Cory. "Hey, how come you aren't moving?"

He said, "Well, they didn't call my name. They just called yours and three others."

Turned out to be me, two Indians, and a black. This seemed fishy, and the old discrimination flag shot up. I said, "How come you named us in funny sequence with a whole bunch of numbers in between left out. There were people sitting on bunks, with numbers lower than mine. Everything is supposed to go according to sequence, and these called numbers seemed to jump around. How come?"

He said, "I have no idea. You're moving now. That's an order! Go back and get your stuff."

I said, "I heard you. You did your part perfectly, and this is not personal about any inefficiency on your part."

"Defying my orders?" he shouted, becoming nearly purple with rage. In order to prevent a potential physical assault, I quickly left his office. Although his ego was bruised, I did not wish for him to be penalized for striking me.

Later, the superintendent called me to his office. He said, "What's the problem?"

I said, "Does this federal institution practice racial discrimination?" It was embarrassing for me to ask that because racism was so rampant in his jail.

But to my surprise, he replied, "Of course not." That gave me the opening to inquire about the nonsequential order to move. As proof, I gave him our twenty sequential names and numbers with circles around the non-white names.

He looked at the list for awhile, then said he wanted to check that out. "Let me study this. I'll call you in later."

About a week later, I was moved to a previously all-white section. And the predominant non-white section was not lily-white after that. However, I thought I would end up in the black hole and that I would have to go on a hunger strike or something.

That incident ended with no penalty, but I was expecting the worst. The black hole was a distinct possibility, and possibly on a diet of bread and water for a few days. After all, disobeying an officer was a serious offense in their eyes. With some of my fellow inmates, we reviewed the possibilities and how best I might face them. As a way of strengthening my psychological posture, while engaging in a bit of one-upmanship, I was prepared not only to quietly enter the black hole but to go on a week's fast, taking only water. Not only would that be good for my spirit; it would defuse the threat of putting me on a bread-and-water punishment. As things turned out, none of this was necessary. In fact, an erstwhile segregation practice regarding dormitories was lifted, and two weeks later, I was placed in what was previously an all-white section.

In prison, you could deteriorate, mentally and morale-wise, so some of us thought of creative ways to protest. My CO colleagues and I worked hard at using good-natured humor. They had a regulation, no beards. One day an officer said to a guy who hadn't been shaving, "Hey you! You've been told many times. Get out of the line, get back there, and shave right now, or you're going to be punished." When the man came back, he looked funny. He shaved everything off—eyebrows, etc. We all had a good laugh, and finally some of the officers laughed, too. One of the most demoralizing things in prison is that they take away the prisoners' ability to make decisions. One of the ways we tried to combat that was to initiate things so we were practicing some level of decision making. That also included making a decision to conform to the laws instead of violating them; that's a decision that we made, so we weren't just conforming automatically.

On one occasion, one of the guys refused to do something and was sent down into the hole. A relative of his contacted Norman Thomas, who sent a letter of inquiry to the Bureau of Prisons asking for the facts of the situation. The Bureau of Prisons sent a wire to McNeil, saying, "What's this query we got from a prominent person in New York?" Well, the guy came right out of that hole!

McNeil Island had a main penitentiary and a farm camp, Dupont, about three miles off on another part of the island. The dormitories were huge halls with double bunks lined up. I was on the farm with a system of control called "the count." Every couple of hours, a whistle would blow, and wherever you were assigned, you'd stop and move to a visible place so the officers could count you. When the count was over, the whistle would blow, and you'd go back to your activities.

On the farm, about a third of us were wartime prisoners, religious people, and conscientious objectors, those who fouled up on the Selective Service System. There were a lot of people from Alaska, which was a federal territory at that time, and men from Indian reservations, as these were all federal cases. I met an Issei there who was involved in some kind of murder rap, who had been there for about twenty-five years. I never did find out what issues were involved, but he was the gentlest person.

In the main prison, there were the Minidoka (WRA camp) no-no boys. As long as the WRA kept their families incarcerated, these men were answering "no" to questions 27 and 28. There were thirty to forty Heart Mountain (WRA camp) no-no boys with me on the farm camp. I knew a lot of the Minidoka boys since they were from Seattle, and I used to see them occasionally when I went to the main line. I played baseball with the farm boys, and they were mostly from the San Francisco Bay area and Los Angeles.

In my first public address after release from prison, I made the front page of a Seattle daily by recommending that all judges should serve a sentence of ninety days in prison, incognito, as a requirement for serving on the bench.

The Postwar Years and Vindication

GORDON DID NOT CONTINUE TO KEEP A PERSONAL DIARY AFTER the war. Nor did he systematically save his own letters or save letters written to him. This obviously makes part III somewhat different in tone and format from parts I and II.

Part III begins by quoting from an unpublished document that we found in Gordon's files, summarizing his educational and professional trajectory after the war. In short order, he finished his bachelor's, master's, and doctoral degrees before accepting a series of professorial jobs in the Middle East. Throughout this period, immediately after the war, Gordon continued to reflect on peace and social justice issues. These would not only continue to resonate in terms of his dissatisfaction with the outcome of his legal cases from the 1940s but would grow to include his concerns about the Middle East and his eventual involvement in the Japanese Canadian redress movement in the 1980s.

Gordon's thoughts about the vindication represented by the successful conclusion of his *coram nobis* case more than forty years after the fact are not as detailed as they might have been had he already been retired at the time the challenge began to take shape. Gordon was, in fact, fully occupied while the case unfolded, having chaired the Department of Sociology at the University of Alberta, in Edmonton, Canada, for many years, along with his regular teaching and disciplinary duties. After a long and sometimes taxing battle, there can be little doubt that Gordon was completely sincere when he said, when the court eventually ruled in his favor, "This was truly a people's case, a people's victory, and it was a privilege for me to be a part of it."

Gordon, age twenty-seven, holding his six-month-old twins, Marion and Sharon, Seattle, December 1945. Courtesy of Sharon M. Yuen

Gordon Hirabayashi and his fellow sociology graduate student Keith Griffiths, University of Washington, June 1949. The two men were hired to help carry out a survey of "race relations" in the Seattle metro area. Courtesy of Susan Carnahan

Washington Public Opinion Laboratory, University of Washington, June 1949. From left, seated: Gordon Hirabayashi, sociology graduate student, and Keith Griffiths, sociology teaching associate. Standing: Robert O'Brien, sociology professor; P. Allen Rickles, Seattle attorney and state director of the Anti-Defamation League; and Stuart Dodd, professor and director of the University of Washington Public Opinion Laboratory. Courtesy of Susan Carnahan

The Hirabayashi family, back in Seattle after their time in the Pinedale and Tule Lake camps, summer 1946. From left, front row: Mitsuko, Shungo, and Esther with twin daughters, Sharon and Marion. Back row: Richard, Gordon, Edward, Jim, and Esther (Tosh). Courtesy of James Hirabayashi

Gordon Hirabayashi, around the time he was serving as chair of the
Department of Sociology, University of Alberta, Edmonton, Canada, 1969.
Courtesy of Sharon M. Yuen

CHAPTER 18

Early Postwar Experiences

AFTER FINISHING MY MCNEIL STINT IN 1945, I WAS BACK IN Seattle, and I asked the University of Washington bookstore manager, Ev McRay, if he could get me a job at the bakery across the street. The owner, Marlatt, was a personal friend of McRay's who expressed interest in hiring me. Marlatt noted, however, "I don't think I can get Gordon in because he has to have some experience before he can join the union, and he has to be a union member before I can use him." On the basis that I lacked certified work experience, the union would not accept me. The training and experience I had under my belt from work in the Tucson jail bakery didn't count. The bakery was interested in taking me on, but the union wouldn't budge on this technicality.

I have always been a supporter of labor unions in principle. Their attempts to get workers a fair shake were commendable, but my personal experiences with unions were quite negative. During the war, the Teamsters Union was instrumental in forcing the leading law firm in Seattle to remove its young lawyer who had enthusiastically begun work as my first lawyer.

My return to the university was motivated by a feeling that even if I worked as a truck driver, a degree might come in handy in assuming higher responsibilities in the organization. My sociology professors bent over backward to mitigate the handicaps of discrimination I was carrying. Even though I was only a beginning MA student in 1947, I was selected along with two veterans to become a teaching associate. When I shared this good news with Mary Farquharson, she was flabbergasted but pleased, saying, "A few years ago they put you in prison for your ancestry, labeling you a non-alien, and now they trust you with the education of their children!" Later, as I was not awarded a GI Bill for my prison service, my professors concocted a plan to minimize that disadvantage by giving me a second class to teach, an upper-division course. When a vacancy for an acting instructorship later emerged, I was selected over my otherwise equal colleagues.

In 1951, while working toward my PhD at the University of British Columbia, I was appointed research sociologist on the Doukhobor Research Committee. The Doukhobors—religious immigrants from Russia—took me into their hearts and confidence (to the surprise of my more experienced colleagues) because I was non-white and non-British. Further, I was a non-Canadian at that point, so I was not part of the "persecuting government." It has been my experience since the war that my minority status has frequently turned out to be an advantage, aside from any personal qualities of my own, a positive labeling, so to speak, for a change.

I had always wanted to work overseas, so after getting my PhD in 1952, I accepted an offer from the American University in Beirut, Lebanon, for a three-year term as assistant professor. Because of my huge FBI file, compiled during the war, I received clearance for my passport much earlier than persons without files because the big scare was Communism and Senator Joseph McCarthy was on the warpath. During my second semester in Beirut, I was appointed chair of the Sociology Department, a position that had been vacant for five years. After my term was over, I accepted an offer from the American University in Cairo to serve as assistant director of the Ford Foundation–supported Social Research Center and as a part-time associate professor of sociology.

While I was overseas, I had two kinds of personal experiences that augmented some trends mentioned earlier. In Beirut and Cairo, I was an American or, at times, a Japanese American. So I had the experience of being a genuine, full-blooded American, for better or worse, and have learned to handle that role without any hang-ups or inauthenticity. I found that I don't have to be Anglo or even white to be an American. Yet there were times when others noted my non-white aspect, as in establishing rapport with village leaders while conducting research, and that seemed to relax them more. I mention this to indicate that while I was having the new experience of being a plain old American, I was not pushing racial aspects under the rug. It was always there, a natural part of me, sometimes disadvantageous but increasingly advantageous. The other experience stems from the periodic consulting I did on behalf of the American Friends Service Committee, sometimes to secure clearance and establish understanding of relief projects, sometimes to interview candidates for international seminars in Europe. These gave me new perspectives and appreciation for the importance of integrity in international relations and the contributions of groups like the AFSC toward world peace.

After the 1956 Suez War, field research in the Arab Middle East became more tedious. Various ministry officials would give their personal endorsements and encouragement for my proposed studies but recommend that I seek the signature of some other official. The activities of a social researcher investigating in a community and the activities of the spy are not generally distinguishable, and should one of the approved projects turn out to be directed by a suspected spy, the signing minister would become vulnerable. Few wanted to take that risk. Research therefore frequently turned out to be three-quarters of the time spent on red-tape clearance and one-quarter of the time devoted to actual studies. In 1959, the University of Alberta made an attractive offer, and, encouraged particularly by some of my former professors and erstwhile graduate student colleagues, I signed a two-year initial contract.

At the University of Alberta, I served as chair of the Department of Sociology for seven years during the turbulent 1960s. Enrollment was booming, and recruiting was one of my major tasks along with program development and specializations after opening a PhD program in 1965. When I came to Alberta, I arrived as the second sociologist along with a third. We were thirteen in number when I became the chair. When I stepped down in 1970, we had a staff of thirty-two, with a full-time equivalent (counting part-timers) of forty-five, and approximately eighty graduate students. I was glad to step down and return to teaching and research.

In addition to university functions, I was able to participate in the establishment of the Friendship Center, the first social center for Indians and Métis (Indians of mixed ancestry), and helped set up the first national program on this movement. It was also exciting to be involved in the revival of a national Japanese Canadian program on the occasion of the celebration of the one hundredth anniversary of the first-known Japanese settler in Canada. Since 1976, I have been involved in the Japanese American redress movement and also been a consultant to the emerging Japanese Canadian redress movement.

The 1980s opened a new chapter in my life, with a protracted struggle to overturn my wartime convictions via a little-known legal remedy known as a writ of error *coram nobis*.

Gordon Hirabayashi with Peter Irons's seminal book *Justice at War*. Irons's research was the foundation of three writ of error *coram nobis* cases during the 1980s, one of which resulted in the U.S. government vacating Gordon's wartime conviction. On the wall are some of the honors Gordon received for his principled stand during the war. Courtesy of Sharon M. Yuen

Fund-raising event for Gordon Hirabayashi's *coram nobis* defense, Washington, D.C., 1985. From left: Susan Lee, president of the Asian American Bar Association in Washington, D.C.; Gordon; Congressman Don Edwards; and Congressman Norman Mineta. Courtesy of Sharon M. Yuen

Gordon Hirabayashi (*front*) and defense team, including Rod Kawakami (*second row, left*), Kathryn Bannai (*second row, right*), and Peter Irons (*third row, right*), on the steps of the federal courthouse, Seattle, 1985. Courtesy of Stanley N. Shikuma

Gordon Hirabayashi delivering the commencement address at Michigan State University, where he also received an honorary doctor of humanities degree, East Lansing, March 9, 1991. Courtesy of Sharon M. Yuen

Gordon Hirabayashi holds his Justice in Action award at an Asian American Legal Defense Fund dinner, New York, February 1992. To his right is Asian American lawyer, author, and professor Phil Tajitsu Nash. Courtesy of Sharon M. Yuen

James and Gordon Hirabayashi, Crissy Field, San Francisco, May 16, 1998. Courtesy of Sharon M. Yuen

Gordon Hirabayashi, age ninety-one, Edmonton, Alberta, Canada, April 25, 2009. Courtesy of Sharon M. Yuen

CHAPTER 19

Coram Nobis

IN THE EARLY 1980S, AIKO HERZIG-YOSHINAGA, SENIOR ARCHI-
vist for the Commission on Wartime Relocation and Internment of
Civilians, discovered an original draft of a manuscript written by General John L. DeWitt, *Final Report: Japanese Evacuation from the West
Coast, 1942*. DeWitt's *Final Report* is critically important because, as
it entails the perspective of a senior military commander, it was used
to justify Japanese American removal and incarceration. Although
the draft had supposedly been destroyed four decades earlier, a copy
had somehow escaped the shredder and was lying unfiled on the desk
of an archival clerk. Herzig-Yoshinaga noticed that the original draft
differed from the official version used in my federal court hearings in
1942–43. While the final version stated it would be impossible to separate the "loyal" from the "disloyal" Japanese Americans, the original
draft version declared that the lack of time, because of the wartime
emergency, made mass exclusion the only alternative (the "military
necessity" thesis). The wayward original version played a significant
role in both the *coram nobis* hearings and the Japanese American
redress movement.

Although that discovery was exciting in its own right, a legal historian, Peter Irons, who was researching in the same archive, helped
capitalize on the discovery. He found correspondence in the government files from Edward Ennis, a Justice Department lawyer, who had
prepared the Supreme Court brief to Solicitor General Charles Fahy
regarding a naval intelligence report contradicting the army's claim

of widespread disloyalty among Japanese Americans. The conclusion to Ennis's brief advocated individual loyalty hearings for Japanese Americans instead of mass removal and incarceration. The Justice Department had a duty to advise the court about the existence of this report and that any other course of conduct might approximate the suppression of evidence. Fahy ignored the warning not to withhold these findings on the racial bias of mass incarceration from the Supreme Court, and that is what opened the door to a reconsideration of my 1943 conviction.

Was it just fate that Peter Irons, just one among the only 2 percent of lawyers familiar with *coram nobis*, knew about this rarely used legal device that allows a rehearing to challenge a federal criminal conviction obtained by the government through constitutional or fundamental errors? Irons called me, and I told him, "I've been waiting over forty years for this call." *Coram nobis* wasn't there for us during the war, but along with an extraordinary degree of citizen commitment, and pro bono lawyers, something wonderful happened for justice. It led to our *coram nobis* cases from 1983 to 1987.

The San Francisco *coram nobis* team was looking at all the papers in Dale Minami's office. Peter Irons recommended that they begin with the appeals court where all three cases were processed. He called me, saying that, in contacting Ennis and Fahy and others, they found some evidence of cover-ups. So that, plus the FBI's own statements and FCC's statements, became the big ammunition in appealing our wartime convictions.

In January 1983, after conferring with Irons and his team, Fred Korematsu, Minoru Yasui, and I jointly announced plans to petition for a writ of error *coram nobis* in the respective federal district courts where our wartime convictions had been issued: Korematsu's in San Francisco, Yasui's in Portland, Oregon, and mine in Seattle.

To Victor Stone, U.S. Department of Justice, July 15, 1983. Re *Korematsu v. US*, *Hirabayashi v. US*, *Yasui v. US*: A motion to vacate each of the convictions of the petitioners and a motion to dismiss the indictment or information to the petitioners made by the United States in open court before each of the judges assigned to these respective actions.

My case, the last of the three to get a hearing, involved a change in the Justice Department's strategy. The federal attorneys fought for dismissal on technicalities. They maintained that the time allowed for a petition had expired, and that I should have requested the rehearing forty years earlier. In addition, since I was a successful professor, I obviously had not suffered from the wartime convictions and therefore did not qualify for a *coram nobis* petition.

I submitted an affidavit in support of the reply to government's response and motion to the U.S. District Court, Western District of Washington, Seattle. I wrote, "I believe that acquiescing to the exclusion order would be giving helpless consent to the denial of democratic principles for which this nation stands, and it is a violation of the Christian principles that give me the incentive to live."

Judge Voorhees turned down the government's request to throw out my lawsuit, saying, "The man is seeking vindication of his honor, and I feel that he has that right."

The stand I took in 1942 was important to the extent that there were people behind me in Seattle and also around the country. As time went on, the numbers grew. When we had our rehearing forty years later, we found young Asian American lawyers taking charge. In my case, they were Kathryn Bannai, Rodney Kawakami, Benson Wong, and Michael Leong. One said, "My dad's no longer living and he lost everything. This is one way to vindicate him." Another said, "Many of us work in the legal profession, [and with your case] we have the privilege of being a part of this important Supreme Court issue. We are working pro bono but getting a lot of benefit from it."

I was not directly involved with the *coram nobis* legal defense since I am not a lawyer. I stayed in touch and raised questions when there were policy decisions to be made. Initially, they were going to contest the removal issue. My original Quaker lawyer, Art Barnett, wanted to include the curfew issue, saying it was bad in principle to omit it from consideration. So I told him to discuss this with the *coram nobis* lawyers, and they had several meetings but he didn't bring that up. Barnett said, "I like those guys. They worked so hard and I respect them." He had them over to his Bainbridge Island home. They came with their families and had a good time digging for oysters because Barnett's wife, Virginia, annually got seeds from Japan. He reiterated, "I respect them so much that I don't want to sound like a consultant sitting on the sidelines and not working as they did. I don't want to sound like I'm criticizing them." So I told him that I was going to talk to them and tell them that he had a concern, and, lawyer to lawyer, they ought to listen to that.

At some point, they said to me, "We're appealing that. We're accepting this major decision . . . we're appealing the curfew issue because it ought to be done the same way."

Art said to them, "You have produced a powerful brief, so carefully grounded and referenced. You have also managed to insert the government's reliance of judicial notice and Gordon's deprivation of constitutional guarantees during the 1942 trial. My sincere appreciation to all of you. I am proud to be a part of this great endeavor with you."

I drafted a statement to Judge Voorhees for the *coram nobis* procedure.

> Your Honor, my name is Gordon Hirabayashi. I am the Petitioner in this case. . . . During World War II, I had the Constitution to protect me. Nevertheless, I was sent to prison for trying to live like other Americans. Other Americans of Japanese ancestry were uprooted and detained in concentration camps en masse, purely on the basis of their ancestry. While constitutional guarantees existed in 1942–43, public institutions did not have the will nor the inclination to uphold them.
>
> It was devastating to me to witness my government committing act after act, stripping me of my constitutional rights. Because of the stand I took in 1942, I have continuously had to defend my actions and prove my loyalty. More than that, the government was crucially involved in the gross violation of my constitutional guarantees. In fact, the government was so intent upon maintaining

the exclusion orders that it withheld information from the Supreme Court that questioned military necessity and similar misconduct.

At my district court trial in October 1942, Judge Black gave this instruction to the jury:

> You can forget all that discussion about the Constitution by the Defense. Your responsibility is to take account of the Curfew and Exclusion Orders issued by the Western Defense Command. Accordingly, you are to determine whether the defendant is of Japanese ancestry; if he is, you are to determine whether he had violated the Curfew Orders and whether he had registered and left for camp as instructed. If he had failed to do any of these orders, you are to return a verdict of guilty.

I responded:

> Your Honor, I have wondered ever since whether I was given an adequate trial from a constitutional perspective. But I wasn't really concerned, because I was confident that when the case got to the Supreme Court, I would be vindicated. I was to receive another rude shock. With one vacancy on the Supreme Court at that time, I lost 8–0. Not a single Supreme Court justice supported my effort to uphold our Constitution.
>
> We have filed a petition for a writ of error *coram nobis* because I had felt that the Supreme Court decision was a black mark on constitutional law. As a citizen, I considered it my responsibility to contribute toward the establishment of respect and honor for our Constitution. Moreover, I wish to have the United States continue to be regarded as a model for democracy, particularly among the newly emerging countries in the Third World where I researched and taught during the first decade of my professional career. It was ironic that while I, among others, brought to these areas the attractions of American democracy, they wanted to know why America would imprison its own citizens for being of a particular ancestry.

With great effort I was able to make a positive response, declaring my continuing faith in the American system of justice and my belief that there would come a day when the injustice suffered would be acknowledged and the convictions overturned.

During the hearing, I told Judge Voorhees that I received an anonymous letter dated October 1982. It was signed "A Japanese Friend and I hope it will always be thus!" The letter reads:

Maybe our government did irrational things . . . so did your people when they attacked the Islands. . . . This was war and during such a confrontation one can expect bizarre solutions to problems. . . . Have you forgotten how the US Government helped Japan to reestablish itself as a world power? . . . Can't you find anything to be grateful for, or is your ambition cloistered in a desire to get even no matter what the consequences?

[Gordon went on to comment:]

Your Honor, this is a letter written not forty years ago during the war but in the 1980s. Note: This letter characterizes me as an Imperial Japanese subject, ungrateful for all the good things America has done for Japan. This view is representative of more people than I think America deserves, so a continued effort must be made to enlighten all Americans of the precious commodity that our Constitution is. . . . I cannot understand how our government continues in this day to defend violations of our Constitution and not acknowledge our petition in the interest of justice.

When confronted with the option of obeying the government orders or violating them, I had no choice but to disobey. My whole philosophy of life and motive to maintain good citizenship demanded that I uphold the constitutional guarantees. . . . What good are principles, if we suspend them each time there is a crisis? This is not only my case, this is not only a Japanese American case— this is an American case. Can it happen again? Yes. It is vitally important to ensure that bizarre solutions have less opportunity to occur again. On the personal side, Your Honor, I have filed the petition to clear my name of the stigma of questionable loyalty to the United States. I believe it is important to assume active responsibilities of citizenship.

My citizenship is something I deeply cherish. In conclusion, I would ask the government why it continues to this day to defend violations of our Constitution and not acknowledge my petition in the interests of justice. Thank you, Your Honor.

Aiko Herzig-Yoshinaga told me that the judge spent all morning quizzing her in detail about how they find things in the archives. Aiko said, "The system is like this. You locate things that are already filed, but there are a lot of things still in cartons and there are things not filed properly." The DeWitt article was lying on the desk of one of the archivists, and she noticed it. "Gee, this version is different from the official one!" And it dawned on her that the copy she was looking at had escaped the shredder for some reason and was not filed. So she made some copies, and she got so excited she couldn't sleep when she realized what it was. She needed to tell somebody, so she showed it to Peter Irons. Peter got excited because he knew that in certain rare circumstances, a discovery of this nature that completely contradicts the government's position could be grounds for a new trial, even after forty years, via this rarely used legal device "writ of error *coram nobis*."

Peter Irons was very good. He's articulate and he's got a photographic memory. When the government started to probe him, he set 'em on their heels, so they didn't ask him very many things.

I met Edward Ennis at my hearing. In a 1944 memo, Ennis, head of the [World War II] Alien [Enemy] Control unit of the U.S. attorney's office in Washington, wrote to Assistant Attorney General Herbert Wechsler: "It is highly unfair to this racial minority that these lies being put out in official publications go uncorrected."

One of our lawyers, Rod Kawakami, secured a deputation—an authenticated, legalized interview that could be used as testimony—

as we didn't know when the trial would be and whether Ennis would be free or able to come because of his health. He was cooperative and gave a very supportive interview. He said, "If you want me to appear as a live witness, I would be pleased to come."

At the trial, the star witness that we introduced who really made an impact was Ennis. He recalled, "Oh yes, we were aware that the FBI had said they'd picked up everybody and it wasn't necessary to move every soul, kids and women—everybody." J. Edgar Hoover had already ordered them to pick up anybody who was suspicious. Ennis wrote the brief that Fahy, the solicitor general, presented; but none of this was in the final brief. Ennis said, "This is a case where the government violated the Constitution, and they knew it."

Judge Voorhees ruled that it was not reasonable for me to have had access to the relevant documents before the 1980s; thus the time allowed for a petition should fall within that period. Judge Voorhees ruled at the end of 1987:

> It is now here ordered and adjudged by this Court that the judgment of the said District Court as to the exclusion conviction is affirmed. The judgment as to the curfew conviction is reversed and the matter is remanded with instructions to grant Hirabayashi's petition to vacate both convictions.

Judge Voorhees's comment on his decision was "Injustices occur from time to time. In a democracy, if citizens care enough and are patient enough, there will come an opportunity to overturn the injustice." So although my exclusion conviction stood, I had won my case regarding curfew.

Subsequent to Judge Voorhees's decision, I can do no better than to quote my legal team's statement following the decision:

> The Hirabayashi legal team hails Judge Donald Voorhees' decision as a clear victory for and complete vindication of those of Japanese American descent who suffered the hardships, humiliation

and indignities of the uprooting and internment during World War II. . . . In reading Judge Voorhees' decision, several key points emerge: (1) The Petition was granted to avoid the perpetuation of a "manifest injustice"; (2) the manifest injustice involved the government misleading the Court into justifying the "evacuation" of the Japanese American population on the basis of suppressed evidence; (3) were it not for the suppression, it would have been very difficult for the government to advance to the Supreme Court its justification for the exclusion, a justification which ultimately became the basis of the Supreme Court decision; (4) and finally, the suppression of evidence involved governmental misconduct of such a fundamental character that Gordon Hirabayashi was denied his due process rights to a fair hearing which therefore mandated the action of the exclusion conviction.

We appealed the exclusion point in the U.S. District Court, Western District of Washington, January 13, 1988. Pursuant to the mandate of the U.S. Court of Appeals for the Ninth Circuit in this case, the petitioner's conviction on Count II of his indictment is hereby set side. The Court set aside the petitioner's conviction on Count I of his indictment prior to his appeal. As to whether I was suffering, the U.S. Ninth Circuit Court of Appeals found in my favor on September 24, 1988. "A United States citizen who is convicted of a crime on account of race is lastingly aggrieved."

I did not regret my wartime decision to stand for my rights. In my own appraisal of the meaning of citizenship in our Constitution, the only realistic position available to me was an idealistic one. Anything else would have been the destruction of my self-respect, my values, my beliefs—the necessary ingredients that make up a good citizen.

Why did I cling to the constitutional values in spite of the wartime injustices? It wasn't the Constitution that failed me. It was those entrusted to uphold it who failed me. In times of crises, when the usual sources of direction and "landmarks" for decision making aren't available, what constitutes realistic, practical behavior? What role does idealism play in such circumstances? Sailing through uncharted waters, what becomes realism? The answers to these questions are not easy. But one needs something more than the truism that "idealism" is all right, but in a crisis one must be "realistic." In fact, my story illustrates that in a crisis, the opposite formula may be just as true.

I would add that the fact that the courts vacated my convictions more than forty years after the fact is not only a victory for me personally, nor just for the Japanese Americans. It is a great victory for all Americans. The twelve volunteer lawyers, the large number of citizen committees that embarked on public education (how can people be upset about something they don't know about?), and the many supporters who donated funds to enable the essential work during the 1980s, all helped to rescue this case from obscurity in the archives. This was truly a people's case, a people's victory, and it was a privilege for me to be a part of it.

APPENDIX 1

Major Publications

Hirabayashi, Gordon. "Departmental Chairman or Chore-Boy?" *The Pacific Sociological Review* 13, no. 1 (Winter 1970): 14–16.

———. "50 Years Later: Where Do We Go from Here?" *Friends Journal* 38, no. 11 (1992): 35.

Hirabayashi, Gordon, and Lincoln Armstrong. "Social Differentiation in Selected Lebanese Villages." *American Sociological Review* 21, no. 4 (August 1956): 425–34.

Hirabayashi, Gordon, B. Y. Card, and C. French. *The Metis of Alberta Society.* Edmonton, Canada: University of Alberta Press, 1963.

Hirabayashi, Gordon, A. Cormier, and V. Billows. *The Problem of Assisting Aboriginal Canadians to Urban Adjustment.* Toronto: Indian-Eskimo Association, 1962.

Hirabayashi, Gordon, and May Ishaq. "Social Change in Jordan: A Quantitative Approach in a Non-census Area." *The American Journal of Sociology* 64, no. 1 (July 1958): 36–40.

Hirabayashi, Gordon, and M. Fathalla El Khatib. "Communication and Political Awareness in the Villages of Egypt." Special issue, *The Public Opinion Quarterly* 22, no. 3 (Autumn 1958): 357–63.

Hirabayashi, Gordon, and Neil Lindquist. "Coping with Marginal Situations: The Case of Gay Males." *The Canadian Journal of Sociology / Cahiers Canadiens de Sociologie* 4, no. 2 (Spring 1979): 87–104.

Hirabayashi, Gordon, and H. el-Saaty. *Industrialization in Alexandria: Some Social and Ecological Aspects.* Cairo: American University Press, 1959.

Hirabayashi, Gordon, with P. A. Saram. "Conceptions of Happiness and Aspirations for Change." *Journal of Asian and African Studies* 13, nos. 3–4 (1978): 265–71.

Hirabayashi, Gordon, and K. V. Ujimoto. *Asian Canadian in Multicultural Canada*. Guelph, Ontario, Canada: University of Guelph, 1980

———. *Asian Canadian Symposium*. Vols. 1–3. Guelph, Ontario, Canada: University of Guelph, 1977–79.

———. *Asian Canadians: Regional Perspectives*. Guelph, Ontario, Canada: University of Guelph, 1982

———. *Visible Minorities and Multiculturalism: Asians in Canada*, Toronto: Butterworths, 1980

Professional Positions, Honors, and Awards

1947–51	Teaching associate, University of Washington
1951–52	Acting instructor, University of Washington
1952–54	Assistant professor, American University of Beirut, Lebanon
195–55	Associate professor, American University of Beirut
1955–59	Associate professor, American University in Cairo, Egypt
1959	Associate professor, University of Alberta, British Columbia
1963	Vice President, Western Association of Sociology and Anthropology
1964	President, Western Association of Sociology and Anthropology
1979–81	Vice President, Canadian Ethnic Studies Association
1981–83	Member of the board of directors, Canadian Ethnic Studies Association
1982	LLD (doctor of laws) degree, Honoris Causa, Haverford College, Pennsylvania
Dec. 4, 1983	Bill of Rights Day Celebration, San Francisco
1983	Co-recipient, Earl Warren Civil Liberties Award, Northern California Foundation, American Civil Liberties Union, San Francisco
1983	Earl Warren Civil Liberties Award, American Civil Liberties Union of Northern California

1984	LHD (doctor of humane letters) degree, Honoris Causa, Hamline
	University, Saint Paul, Minnesota, and LLD (doctor of laws), Honoris Causa, Haverford College, Pennsylvania
Dec. 4, 1986	Selection to the Washington State Centennial Hall of Honor, Washington State Historical Society, Tacoma, Washington
Mar. 9, 1991	HD (doctor of humanities) degree, Michigan State University, East Lansing, Michigan
Jan. 30, 1992	Justice in Action award, Asian American Legal Defense and Education Fund
1992	Commemorative Medal for the 125th Anniversary of the Confederation of Canada
1993	Distinguished Service Award, Western Oregon State College (from 1995, Western Oregon University), Monmouth, Oregon, and Courage Award, Washington State Trial Lawyers Association, Seattle, Washington (co-recipient with Art Barnett)
1994	Festschrift, *Status and Identity in a Pluralistic Society: Essays in Honor of Gordon K. Hirabayashi*, edited by P. Krishnan. Delhi: BR Publishing.
1998	Doctor of Arts, Honoris Causa, University of Lethbridge, Alberta, Canada
1999	Catalina Honor Camp in the Coronado National Forest, Arizona, where
	Gordon served his sentence of hard labor, renamed the Gordon Hirabayashi Recreation Site
May 9, 2000	Celebration of Distinction, Seattle City Council, Resolution 301767, recognizing Gordon Hirabayashi for his acts of courage resisting unjust laws, efforts to eliminate social injustice, and steadfast commitment to constitutional rights for all
May 9, 2000	Seattle City Council, Resolution 30177, honoring Gordon Hirabayashi for his commitment to social justice and his career as a world-renowned social scientist, humanist, and human rights activist

May 2002	University of Washington establishes the Gordon Hirabayashi Endowed Professorship for the Advancement of Citizenship
Oct. 2002	University of Alberta Department of Sociology establishes the Dr. Gordon Hirabayashi Graduate Scholarship in Sociology
Oct. 4, 2002	Asian Pacific Islander Legal Outreach: Community Impact Award. Scholarship created in honor of Gordon Hirabayashi by the Department of Sociology, University of Alberta
2008	The University of Washington awards honorary *nunc pro tunc* (now for then) degrees to four hundred former students of Japanese ancestry whose schooling was interrupted during World War II, including Gordon Hirabayashi.
2012	Presidential Medal of Freedom

Glossary of Names

IN HIS DIARIES AND PERSONAL CORRESPONDENCE, GORDON
Hirabayashi made many references to people who might not be familiar to readers today. This glossary provides the names and titles or
affiliations of select individuals mentioned in the book.

Roger Baldwin, national director, American Civil Liberties Union
Arthur Barnett, Quaker, Gordon Hirabayashi's lawyer
Ernest Besig, director, American Civil Liberties Union of Northern Califor-
 nia
Lloyd D. Black, judge, Gordon Hirabayashi trials
John L. DeWitt, general, Western Defense Command
Delos C. Emmons, general, replaced DeWitt as head of the Western Defense
 Command in 1943
Edward J. Ennis, general counsel of the Immigration and Naturalization
 Service, head of the Alien Enemy Control Unit
Harold Evans, prominent Philadelphia lawyer, Quaker, Gordon Hirabayas-
 hi's Supreme Court lawyer
Charles Fahy, solicitor general, head of the War Division of the U.S. Justice
 Department
Mary Farquharson, University District congressperson, Gordon Hirabayas-
 hi's advocate
Caleb Foote, distinguished scholar and pacifist
Felix Frankfurter, Supreme Court justice
John Geisness, Gordon Hirabayashi's lawyer, partner in Vanderveer law
 firm, withdrew from the case
J. Edgar Hoover, director, Federal Bureau of Investigation
Peter Irons, political science professor at the University of California, San
 Diego

Robert H. Jackson, Supreme Court justice

Rodney Kawakami, lawyer for Gordon Hirabayashi's writ of error *coram nobis* case

Edward Kimmel, colonel, director of the Reserve Officers Training Corps at the University of Washington

Fred Korematsu, resisted mass incarceration, one of the three cases, along with Gordon Hirabayashi's and Minoru Yasui's, that reached the U.S. Supreme Court

Bill Makino, Gordon Hirabayashi's roommate at the University of Washington

Francis V. Manion, FBI Special Agent in Seattle

Dale Minami, lawyer for Fred Korematsu's writ of error *coram nobis* case

Homer Morris, member of the American Friends Service Committee, Philadelphia

Frank Murphy, Supreme Court justice

A. J. Muste, renowned pacifist and social activist

Robert O'Brien, dean, Department of Arts and Sciences, University of Washington

Marilyn Hall Patel, judge, Fred Korematsu's writ of error *coram nobis* case

Allan Pomeroy, assistant U.S. attorney, Gordon Hirabayashi's 1942 trial, Seattle

Stanley Reed, U.S. Supreme Court justice

Eleanor Ring, Gordon Hirabayashi's classmate and supporter

Reverend Ray Roberts, Methodist minister, YMCA administrator

Wiley Rutledge, U.S. Supreme Court justice

Esther Schmoe, Floyd Schmoe's daughter and Gordon Hirabayashi's first wife

Floyd Schmoe, University of Washington biology professor, Quaker activist and director of the American Friends Service Committee, Seattle

Mary Schroeder, judge, Gordon Hirabayashi's writ of error *coram nobis* case

Victor Stone, U.S. Justice Department lawyer in Gordon Hirabayashi's, Fred Korematsu's, and Minoru Yasui's writ of error *coram nobis* cases

Uchimura Kanzo, Japanese Christian and proponent of Mukyokai, or non-church Christianity

George F. Vanderveer, head of prominent Seattle firm

Donald Voorhees, judge, Gordon Hirabayashi's writ of error *coram nobis* case

Frank L. Walters, Gordon Hirabayashi's lawyer, 1942 trial, Seattle

Earl Warren, California state attorney general, elected governor in 1943

Abraham Lincoln Wirin, lawyer, American Civil Liberties Union of Southern California, Wakayama, Fred Korematsu, Gordon Hirabayashi, and Minoru Yasui appeals

M. D. Woodbury, director of the YMCA at the University of Washington

Minoru Yasui, resisted curfew and mass incarceration, one of the cases, along with Gordon Hirabayashi's and Fred Korematsu's, that reached the U.S. Supreme Court

Further Reading

American Friends Service Committee. *Speak Truth to Power: A Quaker Alternative to Violence.* 1955. http://www.quaker.org/sttp.html.

Caldarola, Carlo. *Christianity: The Japanese Way.* Leiden: E. J. Brill, 1979.

Commission on the Wartime Relocation and Internment of Civilians. *Personal Justice Denied.* Washington, DC: U.S. Government Printing Office, 1982.

Concentration Camps, North America: Japanese in the United States and Canada during World War Two. Melbourne, FL: Kreiger, 1981.

Daniels, Roger. *The Decision to Relocate the Japanese Americans.* Philadelphia: Lippincott, 1975.

Drinnon, Richard. *Keeper of Concentration Camps: Dillon Myer and American Racism.* Berkeley: University of California Press, 1987.

Fisher, Anne Reeploeg. *Exile of a Race.* Kent, WA: F. de T. Publishers, 1965.

Flewelling, Stan. *Shirakawa: Stories from a Pacific Northwest Japanese American Community.* Auburn, WA: White River Valley Museum, 2002.

Foote, Caleb. *Outcasts! The Story of America's Treatment of Her Japanese American Minority.* 1943. http://content.cdlib.org/ark:/13030/hb2c60042p.

Hirabayashi, Gordon. *Good Times, Bad Times: Idealism Is Realism.* Sunderland P. Gardner Lecture, Canadian Quaker Pamphlet, No. 22. Argenta, BC: Argenta Friends Press, 1985.

Hohri, William Minoru. *Repairing America: An Account of the Movement for Japanese American Redress.* Pullman: Washington State University Press, 1988.

Ichioka, Yuji. *The Issei: The World of the First Generation Japanese Immigrants, 1885–1924.* New York: Free Press, 1988.

———, ed. *Views from Within: The Japanese American Evacuation and*

Resettlement Study. Los Angeles: Resource Development and Publications, Asian American Studies Center, University of California at Los Angeles, 1967.

Irons, Peter. *Justice at War: The Story of the Japanese American Internment Cases.* New York: Oxford University Press, 1983.

Japanese Consulate, San Francisco. *Japanese Alien Land Law Cases.* Vols. 1 and 2. Washington, DC: Japanese Consulate, 1930.

Kang, Jerry. "Dodging Responsibility: The Story of *Hirabayashi v. United States.*" In *Race Law Stories,* edited by Rachael F. Moran and Devon W. Carbado. New York: Norton, 2008.

Muller, Eric. "*Hirabayashi* and the Invasion Evasion." *North Carolina Law Review* 88, no. 4 (2010):1333–88.

Niiya, Brian. *Japanese Americans during World War II: A Selected Annotated Bibliography of Materials Available at UCLA.* Los Angeles: UCLA, 1992.

Nishinori, John. "Japanese Farms in the State of Washington." Master's thesis, University of Washington, 1926.

Oldham, Kit. "Schmoe, Floyd W. (1895–2001)." 2010. http://www.historylink.org/index.cfm?DisplayPage=output.cfm&file_id=3876.

Pacific Coast Branch, American Friends Service Committee. Information Bulletin: Japanese-American Relations Committee. 1942–46. http://content.cdlib.org/view?docId=ft6b69n9gt&brand=calisphere&doc.view=entire_text.

Reischauer, Edwin, and Marius Jansen. *The Japanese Today: Change and Continuity.* Cambridge, MA: Harvard University Press, 1995.

Schmoe, Floyd. "Seattle's Peace Churches and Relocation." In *Japanese Americans: From Relocation to Redress,* edited by Roger Daniels, Sandra C. Taylor, and Harry H. L. Kitano. 2d ed. Seattle: University of Washington Press, 1991.

Shinkokyo, *The New Homeland.* Journal published by the Issei community in 1900–1910, Seattle, Washington.

Tanaka, Chester. *Go for Broke: A Pictorial History of the Japanese American 100th Infantry Battalion and the 442nd Regimental Combat Team.* Richmond, CA: Go for Broke, 1982.

Tateishi, John, ed. *And Justice for All: An Oral History of the Japanese American Detention Camps.* New York: Random House.

Weglyn, Michi. *Years of Infamy: The Untold Story of America's Concentration Camps.* New York: William Morrow, 1976.

Wilber, Theodore. "American Friends Service Committee Efforts to Aid Japanese American Citizens during World War II." Master's thesis, Boise State University, 2009.

About the Coauthors

JAMES A. HIRABAYASHI (1926–2012), son of hardworking immigrant farmers in the Pacific Northwest and brother of Gordon Hirabayashi, was a high school senior in 1942 when he was detained in the Pinedale Assembly Center before being transferred to the Tule Lake Concentration Camp in Northern California. After World War II, he earned his BA and MA degrees in anthropology from the University of Washington and his PhD from Harvard University. At the time of his death, he was professor emeritus at San Francisco State University, where he had been dean of the nation's first School of Ethnic Studies at SF State. He also held research and teaching positions at the University of Tokyo; the University of Alberta, Edmonton; and Ahmadu Bello University, Zaria, Nigeria.

LANE RYO HIRABAYASHI is a core faculty member of the Department of Asian American Studies at the University of California, Los Angeles (UCLA), where he is also the inaugural George and Sakaye Aratani Professor in Japanese American Incarceration, Redress, and Community. After graduating with honors in 1974 from the Hutchins School of Liberal Studies at Sonoma State University, California, Lane received an MA degree (1976) and a PhD degree (1981) in sociocultural anthropology from the University of California, Berkeley. Subsequently, he held a postdoctoral fellowship at UCLA's Asian American Studies Center in 1981–82. He is author and editor of nine books and anthologies and author/coauthor of more than thirty scholarly articles, the latest of which is "Carlos Bulosan's Final Defiant Acts: Achievements during the McCarthy Era," in *Amerasia Journal* 38 (2012): 29–50.

Index

Page numbers in boldface type indicate photographs.

abatement, plea for, 69, 117, 124
"Accused Jap-American to Marry
    Quaker Girl" (*Washington Star*), 101
ACLU. *See* American Civil Liberties
    Union
AFSC. *See* American Friends Service
    Committee
Alien Enemy Control unit, 187
Alien Land Law (Washington State,
    1923), 17
American Civil Liberties Union
    (ACLU), xiii, 71, 72, 142, 143, 147
American Friends Service Committee
    (AFSC), 44, 58, 92, 93, 94, 95, 97, 99,
    100, 139, 162; Japanese Americans
    and, 51; working for, 53, 137, 145,
    175
American University of Beirut, 174
American University of Cairo, 174
Andrews, Reverend, 31, 50
appeals process, described, 127–28
Arai, Clarence, 116
Arthur D. Jones Real Estate Company,
    140, 141
"As I See Religion" (Fosdick), 156
Auburn Christian Fellowship (ACF), 31
Auburn High School, 31, **35**, 43
Ault, Harry, 138

bail, 73, 88, 89, 127, 162; posting, 69,
    137
Bainbridge Island, xii, 63
baking crew, 151, 154, 1/3
Baldwin, Roger, 71, 72
Bannai, Kathryn, **178**, 183
Baptists, 31, 50, 65
Barnett, Arthur, xiii-xiv, 45, 58, 71,
    120, 184; *coram nobis* and, 183;
    defense committee and, 70; FBI
    and, 66; visit from, 94
Barnett, Virginia, 45, 58, 71, 184
Barney (guard), described, 73–74
Bartley, Bruce, 87
Bechtol, Mr., 31
Bernard, Earl, 123
Besig, Ernest, 72
Between Tears and Laughter (Lin), 107,
    156
bicultural norms, 32–34
Biddle, Francis, 129
Bill of Rights, 34, 45, 63, 68, 72, 103,
    104, 110
Black, Lloyd L., 124, 134, 137; instruc-
    tions from, 125–26, 185; statements
    by, 118–19
Blom, Helen: subpoena for, 120
Booth, G. Raymond, 94
Bowen, Judge, 90

Boy Scouts, 3, 29, 31, 32, 36

Brethren Service Committee, 108

Bridges, Jim, 117

Bureau of Prisons, 126, 150, 152;
    Thomas letter to, 165

Burke, S. J., 143; threats by, 141, 14

Camp Harmony, 88, 115

Campus Christian Council, 96

Captains' Conference of North West
    Squad, 36

Cardozo, Benjamin, 123

career, postwar, 167, 174–76

Cascade Locks camp, 60, 94, 107

Catalina Federal Honor Camp, serving
    time at, 54, 150–59

Catholic Church, conscientious objec-
    tors and, 111

Catholic Hospital, 142

checks-and-balances system, xv, 134

Chin, Frank, xvii

Christian Century, 156

Christianity, 11, 13, 14, 17, 18, 27,
    30–32, 79–80, 108, 110; personality
    and, 156

Christmas card, **98**

Church of the People, 71

citizenship, xiii, 29, 160; active respon-
    sibilities of, 187; Constitution
    and, 189; descent and, 105, 108;
    first-class, 34, 48–50, 57; ignoring,
    69, 108, 117; maintaining, 121, 186;
    native birth and, 130; registration
    of, 161; second-class, 33, 34, 49, 57

Civilian Conservation Corps camp, 150

Civilian Exclusion Order No. 57: xiv,
    58, 107, 125

Civilian Public Service (CPS), 113, 153

Civilian Public Service camps, 60, 107,
    108, 109, 111, 113, 153, 154, 161

civil liberties, 63, 64, 70, 71, 123

Civil War amendments, 103

Clark, William, 13

Commission on Wartime Relocation
    and Internment of Civilians, 181

concentration camps, 51, 58, 103, 127,
    160; American-style, xiii; army
    notices at, 109

Confucius, 14

Connelly, District Attorney, 145

conscientious objector camps, 111–12,
    113, 163

conscientious objectors (COs), 55,
    56, 94, 99, 109, 113, 151, 152, 154,
    160–61, 162; Catholic Church and,
    111; humor of, 165; noncooperation
    by, 157; Social Security Act and, 157

Convictions, 30, 126; challenging, 182;
    vacating, 190

COs. *See* Conscientious objectors
    (COs)

Costigan, Giovanni, 45

CPS. *See* Civilian Public Service

Crane, Theodora, 143

curfew, xii-xiii, xiv, 121, 130, 132, 134,
    183; appealing, 184; complying
    with, 62, 126; issuing, 56, 57, 58,
    185; as reasonable protection, 125;
    resisting, 53, 59, 66, 68, 133–34,
    188; unconstitutionality of, 118,
    135; violation of, xv, 54, 68, 69, 126,
    133

Daniels, Roger, xvii, 3

Darrow, Clarence, 72, 123

Days of Our Years (Lin), 156

Deaconness Hospital, 142

Declaration of Independence, 104

democracy, 55, 60, 64, 103, 109, 110,
    116, 161, 185, 188; denial of, 104,
    183; jail, 77; racism and, 32; regard-
    ing, 104–5

Dennis, J. Charles, 128, 161

Denshō, xvii

Department of Justice, 129, 181, 182, 183

Department of Sociology (University of Alberta), working at, 167, 175–76

deportation, 103, 104

Depression, the, 25, 26, 43

descent, citizenship and, 105, 108

DeWitt, John L., xii, 56, 133, 187; curfew/evacuation and, 132; report by, 181

diary, 68, 167; prison entries in, 99–102

diet, prison, 73–75

discrimination, 4, 53, 68, 133, 157, 163, 173; economic, 105; political, 105; racial, 136, 161, 164; social, 105

disloyalty, 56, 90, 104, 181, 182

Divine, Father, 48

Dodd, Stuart, **170**

Douglas, Lloyd, 156

Douglas, William O., evacuation and, 133

Doukhobor Research Committee, 174

draft, resisting, 84

draft boards, 111, 160–61

Dupont farm camp, 84, 165

Eaton, Ralph: subpoena for, 120

Edge, Lester, 141–143

Edison School, 144

Education, 43, 49, 80, 113, 167, 174, 190; prison, 88–89; religious, 50–51

Edwards, Don, **177**

Eighteenth Amendment, 89

Emmons, Delos, 148

Endo (Mitsuye Endo), 135–36

enemy aliens, xiii, 67, 118, 160

Ennis, Edward, 181, 182, 187, 188

Episcopal Peace Fellowship, 95

Erickson, District Attorney, 161

Ernst, Helen, 143

Ernst, Myron, 142, 143

espionage, 118, 133

Etter, Max, 158

Eurasians, fate of, 87

evacuation, 64, 71, 125, 130, 132, 159; court rulings on, 148; justifying, 189; refusing, 63–64; registering for, 63–64, 67; unconstitutionality of, 118

Evangelists, prison services by, 78–79

Evans, Harold, 132

evidence, suppression of, xv, 189

exclusion, 121, 181, 188; justification for, 189; military security and, 135

exclusion order, 57, 64, 185; complying with, 126; due process and, 125; violation of, 69, 126

Executive Order 9066 (1942), xii, xiv, 56, 125, 134

Ex Parte Endo (1944), 135–36

Extracurricular activities, 44, 47–48

Fahy, Charles, 181, 182, 188

Fair Play Committee, 143

Farquharson, Frederick B., 45, 128

Farquharson, Mary, 71, 72, 94, 119, 174; appeal and, 128; bond release and, 129; defense committee and, 69–70; Kiser and, 142–43

FBI, 68, 119, 120, 161, 188; arrest by, 145, 162; files from, 101, 102, 174; interview with, 66–67

Federal Communications Commission (FCC), 182

Fee, Judge, 128, 130

Fellowship of Reconciliation (FOR), 65, 71, 72, 94, 95, 110, 137, 139, 142–44, 151–53

Fergin, Mr., 29

Fifth Amendment, xv, 125, 133
Final Report: Japanese Evacuation from the West Coast (DeWitt), 181
Finch, Mr., 143
First Baptist Church, 96
Foote, Caleb, 94
FOR. *See* Fellowship of Reconciliation
Ford Foundation, 174
Fort Lawton, 67
Fosdick, Harry, 155, 156
4-C classification, 60
4-D classification, 109
4-E classification, 109, 110, 111, 113, 154
Fox, George, 153
Frankfurter, Felix, 133, 134
Fresno Bee, 130
Friendship Center, 176
Friends Journal, 50, 106

Geisness, John, 123
Gentlemen's Agreement (1907–8), 14
German Americans, 103, 104
Gibran, Khalil, 91
Gold, William, 142, 143
Goodenough, Dr., 96
Gordon Hirabayashi Defense Committee, xiv, 123, 147; makeup of, 69–72
Gordon Hirabayashi Recreation Site, 54
Gordon Kiyoshi Hirabayshi v. the United States of America (1987), xiv
Griffiths, Keith, **169**, **170**
guards, described, 73–74

Harborview Hospital, 100
Heart Mountain WRA camp, 138, 166
Herzig-Yoshinaga, Aiko, 181, 187
Hi-Y, 29, 31–32, **35**
Hile, Gerald, 117, 118, 124, 125
Hines, Donna, 93, 94

Hirabayashi, Edward, **24**, 60, 61, 114–15, **171**; on home life, 27–28; visit from, 93
Hirabayashi (Schmoe), Esther, 42, 93, **98**, 138, 139, **171**; divorce of, 54; letter to, 95–96; marriage of, 101, 102
Hirabayashi, Esther Toshiko (Tosh), **171**
Hirabayashi, Gordon Kiyoshi, **24**, **35–40**, **42**, **98**, **169–77**, **178–80**; birth of, 25; divorce of, 54; draft registration card of, 41 (photo); interviews of, xi–xii; marriage of, 101, 102; voice/perspectives of, xvii–xviii
Hirabayashi, Hamao, **6**
Hirabayashi, James, xvi, xvii, **24**, 60, **98**, **171**, **179**; interviews by, xi–xii; oral history and, 3
Hirabayashi, Joe, 160
Hirabayashi, Lane, xii, xvii
Hirabayashi, Marion, **169**, **171**
Hirabayashi (Suzawa), Mitsuko, **7–9**, 16, **22**, **24**, 95, **97**, **98**, 100, 101, 119, 120, **171**; beauty treatment for, 122; confrontation and, 61; letter from, 114; politics and, 27; reading by, 26–27; subpoena for, 120, 121, 122; support from, 62; trial and, 122; visit with, 147
Hirabayashi, Motoyoshi, **5**, **19**
Hirabayashi, Paul, **25**
Hirabayashi, Richard, **98**, **171**
Hirabayashi, Sharon, **169**, **171**
Hirabayashi, Shungo, **5–7**, 9, 19, 20, **22–24**, 60, **97**, **98**, 119, **171**; honesty of, 26; oral history and, 3; subpoena for, 120, 121, 122; support from, 62; trial and, 124–25; youth of, 11
Hirabayashi, Toshiharu, **5**, **6**, 16, **19**,

20, 24

Hirabayashi family, 3, **5**, **24**, **171**;
Christmas card of, **98**; influence
of, 61–62

"Hirabayashi Taken to McNeil Camp"
(*Seattle Times*), 163

Hirabayashi v. United States (1943), 135,
136, 182

hitchhiking, stories about, 145–49

Holmes, Oliver Wendell, Jr., 123

honesty, 26, 28

Hoover, J. Edgar, 188

Hopis, 153

Horiuchi, Koji, 32

Hosokawa, Bill, 62

Hotaka Club, 12, 15, 16

Housewife's Friend, 26

human personality, violation of, 63–64

hysteria, 105, 132, 134

idealism, role of, 189–90

Iguchi, Kikenji, **8**, 13, 14, 30

Ikeda, Tom, xvii, 3, 93

Iki, Kenji, 76, 115, 116, 120; bail for, 88;
story of, 90–91

incarceration, xv, 53, 67, 69, 70, 73–83,
104, 105, 107, 157–58, 160, 181;
racial bias of, 182; unconstitutionality of, 135

independence, 63, 104, 105

Indians, 86, 151, 163, 165; liquor for,
152; relocation of, 103; social center
for, 176

injustice, 34, 154, 186, 188, 189

integrity, 28, 34, 50, 127, 157

intermarriage, 100, 101, 102

International House, 94

International Young Men's Christian
Association, 35

Invador (yearbook), photo from, **35**

Irons, Peter, xi, xiv, **178**, 181; book by,

177; *coram nobis* and, 182, 187

Issei, 14, 15, 17, 21, 119, 139, 140, 165;
Christianity and, 30; face and, 28;
internment of, 59; naturalizing
and, 58; social context and, 28

Italian Americans, 103; Fascist leagues
of, 104

Jackson, Robert, 136

Jackson Street Boys, described, 82

JACL. *See* Japanese American Citizens
League

jail officials, 77, 81

jails, life in, 73–83, 122

Japan, map of, 12

Japanese aliens, 87; deportation of,
103; discrimination against, 68;
permits for, 148

Japanese American Baptist church, 50

Japanese American Citizens League
(JACL), 62, 115, 147, 160

Japanese-American Courier, 29

Japanese American redress movement, 176, 181

Japanese Americans, 53, 62, 149, 174;
classification of, 60; deportation
of, 103; discrimination against, 68,
104; draft board and, 160; incarceration of, 105, 160, 181; interest/
sympathy toward, 128; loyal/dis-
loyal, 160, 161, 181, 182; removal
of, 90, 134, 181, 184; rights of, 135;
victory for, 190

Japanese Association, 15, 27, 28–29

Japanese Canadian redress movement, 167, 176

Japanese language, shunning, 33

Japanese Students Club, 44, 57, 58

Jarrett, Captain, 74

Jarvis brothers, 31

Jehovah's Witnesses, 85–86, 152

Jensen, Dr., 96
Jesus, believing in, 79–80
Jim Crow laws, challenging, 48
Johnson, Mr., 143
Jones, Mr., 141, 143
Jones, Rufus, 95
Justice at War (Irons), **177**
Justice in Action award, **179**

Kang, Jerry, xvi
Katsuno, Aiko, 17, **20, 22**
Katsuno, Mr., **22**
Katsuno, S., **20, 22**
Kawakami, Rodney, **178**, 183, 187
Kelly, T. R., 106
Kenna, James Brett, 70
Kensei Academy, 8, 13, 14, 15, 16, 30
Kimmel, Colonel, 55, 64, 66–67
King, Herb, 47
King, Martin Luther, Jr., 95
King County Jail, 129, 138; diary
    entries from, 99–102; incarceration
    at, 53, 67, 70, 73–83, 107; jail mates
    at, 84–91; menu at, 74–75; visitors
    to, 92–96
Kiser, Ben, 142–43, 144
Kiyosawa, Fukashi, **6**
Klein, Mrs., 143; threats against, 140,
    141
Korematsu, Fred, xiv, 72, 130, 135, 182
Korematsu v. United States (1944), 135,
    136, 182

Lee, Susan, **177**
Leong, Michael, 183
letters, xvi-xvii, 90, 95–96, 111–13, 123,
    129, 141, 148, 165, 167
Lidgerwood Evangelical Church, 98
Lin Yutang, 107, 156
Lorimer, Allan, 70
Los Angeles Negro Daily, 103

love, 99, 110, 154
loyalty, 58, 160, 181; hearings, 182;
    questionnaire, 54, 161

Madrona Presbyterian, 96
Main Street (Lewis), 156
Makino, Bill, 59, 60, 109
Manion, Francis, 66, 67, 68, 69
marriages, 87, 99, 100, 101, 102
martial law, 63, 71
Martin, Jim, **38, 39**
Maryknoll Registration Center, 67
Massachusetts Agricultural College, 13
materialism, 14, 17, 88, 89
Matsumoto, map of, 12
McCarthy, Joe, 174
McFarland, Bob, **38**
McNeil Island Federal Peniten-
    tiary, 73, 84, 85, 91, 151, 158, 163;
    described, 165; serving time at, 54,
    173
McRae, J. E. (Ev), 71, 173; defense com-
    mittee and, 70
Meditation, 112, 146, 154
Mencius, 14
Merner, Jack, 47, 108–9
Merner, Jean, 47
Métis, social center for, 176
Mexicans, 151, 152
Middle East, concerns about, 167, 175
migration, 14, 103
Milburn, Anna T.: defense committee
    and, 70
Military Area No. 1, 129, 145
Military Area Zone A, 158
military necessity, 124, 132, 133, 134,
    181
Minami, Dale: *coram nobis* and, 182
Mineta, Norman, **177**
Minidoka WRA camp, 87, 115–16, 119,
    120, 140, 141, 165–66

mixed blood, people of, 87
Morris, Edna, 106
Morris, Homer, 94, 106
Morris, Mary, 13
Mott, June, 138
Mukyōkai, 3, 13, 15, 17–18, 23, 30, 31
Muller, Eric, xvi
Multnomah County Jail, 130
Murphy, Frank: dissent and, 133, 135
Murphy, Nora, 17
Murphy, Reverend U. G., 17, 30, 92;
    defense committee and, 70
Muste, A. J., 51
Myers, Mrs. Harry M.: defense com-
    mittee and, 70

Nagano Prefectural Association, 15
Nagano prefecture, 11, 14, 15; map of,
    12
Nash, Phil Tajitsu, **179**
National American Friends Service
    Committee, 71
national security, xv, 56, 71
Negroes, 86, 104, 151, 163; misconcep-
    tions about, 81–82; relocation of,
    103
New York City, 47–48
Nihonjinkai, 15, 28–29
Nisei, 30, 32, 33–34, 58, 82, 87–88, 95,
    103, 110, 118, 120, 130; citizenship
    and, 108; cultural heritage of, 28;
    growing up, 28–29; prejudice and,
    49; removal of, 64, 72; restrictions
    on, 57; socialization of, 34
Nisei *Courier,* 29
Nishinoiri, John Isao, 16–17
"non-alien," xiii, 56, 174
no-no boys, 160, 165–66

O'Brien, Robert, **170**
Okimoto, Mr., 29

Okuda, Kenji, 93, 110
Olmstead, Frank, 51
1-A classification, 113, 154
1-A-O classification, 85
Oraibi Reservation, 153

Pacific Citizen, 147
Pacific Northwest Conference, 95
pacifism, 78, 162; regarding, 107–13
peace, 55, 60, 83, 156, 161, 167
Pearl Harbor, 56, 59, 103, 158
Pegler, Westbrook, 103, 104
persons of Japanese ancestry, xiii;
    discrimination against, 133; evacu-
    ation of, 64, 135; excluding, 58
Peters, Monsignor, 143
Peterson, Rev., 96
"picture bride" custom, 14
Pima County Jail, incarceration at,
    157–58
Pinedale camp, 61, 62, 92
politics, 61–62, 80, 115, 107, 138
Pomeroy, Allen, 124, 125
Pontiac cooperative, 15, 16, **19–22**
prejudice, 48, 49, 86, 104, 107; over-
    coming, 81–82
President's Summer School, **40**, 47, 51
prison, 54, 61, 73, 111; demoralization
    in, 165; deterioration in, 164–65;
    hitchhiking to, 145–49; regula-
    tions, 157; social system and, 81
prisoners: described, 84–91; types of,
    76–77
Proclamations 2 and 3, xiv, 125
profanity, 75, 76, 82
Public Law 503 (1942), xii, 118, 125;
    constitutionality of, 132; violation
    of, xiv, 69
punishment, 157, 164, 165
Puyallup, 67, 69, 87, 88, 89, 90, 115, 116

"Quaker Soul, The" (*Friends Journal*), 50–51

Quakers, xiii, 3, 13, 30, 44, 50, 71, 85, 93, 94, 101, 105, 106, 107, 113, 132, 137, 149, 154, 162; help from, 55, 56, 59; meditation and, 155; service work for, 61

race, 3, 174; misunderstandings based on, 151; relations, survey of, 169

racism, 14, 34, 45, 48, 135, 164; democracy and, 32; regarding, 103–4

Redman, Arthur: defense committee and, 70

Reed, Stanley: evacuation and, 133

Registration, 84, 111, 161

religion, 3, 11, 30–32, 156; regarding, 105–7

removal, xiii, xv, 51, 64, 72, 90, 134, 181, 182, 184

Report of Disposition of Criminal Case (Dept. Circular No. 3429), 162

research, 174–76

resettlement, 139, 140, 141

Revisto, Michael A., 67

Rickles, P. Allen, **170**

rights, 135; constitutional, 71, 184, 185; denial of, 59; due process, 63, 64, 125, 189; human, 33, 64; standing for, 189; suspending, 57

Ring, Eleanor, 94, 117, 120

Ring, Fred, 64, 65, 94

Ring, Mabel, 65

road camps, 126, 145, 150

Road Runner, 151

Robe, The (Douglas), 156

Roberts, Owen: evacuation and, 133

Roberts, Ray, 45, 71; appeal and, 128; bail by, 162; bond release and, 129; defense committee and, 70; testimony of, 162

Rolfsness, Bob, **38**

Roosevelt, Franklin D., 71, 104, 123; curfew/incarceration and, 135; Executive Order 9066 and, xii, 56, 134

Russo-Japanese War (1904), 11

Rustin, Bayard, 51, 95, 107

Rutledge, Wiley: evacuation and, 133

sabotage, 118, 133

Sakamoto, James, 29, 62

Sakata, Jeanne, xvii, 3

Salvation Army, 31

Sand Point Naval Air Base, 15

Sapporo Agricultural College, 13

Sayre, Nevin, 72, 94–95, 137

Schmoe, Floyd, 58, 71, **97**, 101, 142, 143; appeal and, 128; energy/ideas of, 51; personal sacrifice and, 106; release and, 137–38; reunion with, 138–39; subpoena for, 120; visit from, 92, 93; working for, 53

Schmoe, Ruth, **97**, 143

Schmoe, Ruthanna, 93

Schmoe, William (Bill), **42**

Schrock, Mark: resignation of, 108

Schroeder, Mary, xv

Schuyler, George S., 103

Schwellenburg, Louis, 162

Scott, Howard, **38**, 45, 50, 55, 112; classification of, 113; letter from, 111

Scott, Ruane, 112–13

Seattle Draft Board, 160

"Seattle Jap Defies U.S." (*Seattle Post-Intelligencer*), 161

Seattle Post-Intelligencer, 120, 161

Seattle Regional Office, 58

Seattle Times, 96, 120, 163

Section 311, title 50, U.S.C.A. statute, 162

Seelye, Julius H., 13
segregation, 152, 164
Selective Service System, 85, 108, 111, 160, 165
Selective Training and Service Act (1940), 55
self-respect, 61, 189
Shinkokyo, 14–18
Shorter, Fred, 71
Shucklin, Gerald, 67
Shufu no Tomo (magazine), 26
Singer Company, 26
Sino-Japanese War (1894), 11
slavery, 86, 104, 106
Smith, Amy: defense committee and, 70
social action, 50, 51
social clubs, Japanese American, 29
Social justice issues, 167
social Research Center, 174
Socialists, 107
Social Security Act, 157
Society of Friends, 30, 50, 55, 68, 143
spirituality, 3, 14, 18
Spokane Chronicle, 161
Spokane County Jail, 145
Spokane Fellowship of Reconciliation, 142
Stafford, Mr., 90, 116
St. Ann's Church, 143
Steere, Douglas: biographical sketch by, 106–7
stereotypes, Japanese, 15, 126
Stewart, James, 30
Stewart, John, 30
St. Joseph's Hospital, 142
Stone, Harlan, 132, 133–34
Stone, Victor, 182
St. Paul Dispatch, 102
Student Christian Movement, 71
Suez War (1956), 175

Summers, Lane, 91
Suzawa, Mitsuko. *See* Hirabayashi, Mitsuko
Suzuki, Nobu, **97**, 140, 142–43, 144; philosophical view of, 141–42
Suzuki, Paul, **97**, 140, 141, 144; acquaintances for, 142
Suzuki, Yosh, 144
Swedish Hospital, 100

Tajiri, Larry, 147
Takahashi, Ted, 75–76, 93, 115, 117; bail for, 88, 89; education from, 88–89
Tank 3C (Federal Tank), described, 73–74
Teamsters Union, 123, 173
Terminal Island, xii
Testament of Devotion, A (Kelly), 106
Thomas, Evan, 51
Thomas, Norman, 51, 72, 95, 107; letter by, 165
Thomas School, 30
Thomas Union Church, 30
Tojo, Takashi, **5, 20, 22**
Tsuchiya, Henry, 31
Tsuchiya, Takuzo, 32
Tsuneishi, Paul, 3
Tucson, hitchhiking to, 145–49
Tule Lake, camp at, 62, 94, 114, 120, 121

Uchimura, Kanzo, 3, 8, 13, 14, 23, 31; principles of, 30
Union Park District, 141
Unions, 86, 123, 173
Unitarian church, 50, 96
University Book Store, 71
University District, 57, 63
University of Alberta, working at, 167, 175–76

University of British Columbia, studying at, 174

University of Washington, 58; and Hirabayashi, 3, 43–50, 173–74; religious studies at, 50

University of Washington Reserve Officer Training Corps (ROTC), 55, 64, 67

University of Washington YWCA, 45–46, 140

U.S. Army, 109, 129

U.S. Congress, Supreme Court and, 132–33

U.S. Constitution, 34, 45, 47, 121; beliefs about, 70; citizenship and, 189; defending, 62–63, 134, 185; protection from, 108, 127–28; violation of, 63, 68, 104, 118, 134, 186

U.S. Court of Appeals of the Ninth Circuit, xiv, xv, 128–31, 132, 189

U.S. District Court, Western District of Washington, 183, 189

U.S. Marshal's Office, 150

U.S. Public Health, 107

U.S. Supreme Court, xi, xiv, xvi, 123, 124, 129, 145, 148; civil rights cases and, 135; Congress and, 132–33; Constitution and, 134; conviction and, 54; Korematsu and, 130

values, 28, 32, 33–34

"Views & Views" (Schuyler), 103

visitors' days, described, 92–96

Voorhees, Donald S., xv, 183, 186; *coram nobis* and, 184; decision by, 188–89

Walters, Frank, xiv, 93, 119, 124, 129; abatement and, 69, 117; on appeal, 128; brief by, 118; defense committee and, 72, 123; Fifth Amendment and, 125

War Department, 161

War Relocation Authority (WRA), xiii, 62, 87, 94, 139

War Relocation Authority camps, 92, 94, 147; life in, 113–16

War Relocation Center, 107

War Resisters for Peace and Freedom, 51

Wartime Civil Control Administration (WCCA), xii, 53, 67, 94, 115

Wartime Civil Control Administration camp, xiii, 88, 89, 92, 94

Washington Public Opinion Laboratory, **170**

Washington Star, article from, 101

WCCA. *See* Wartime Civil Control Administration

Webster, Daniel, 118

Wechsler, Herbert, 187

wedding, described, 101–2

Western Defense Command, xii, 56, 67, 101, 129, 137, 185; military zones of, 53; public proclamation by, 125–26

Western Washington Fairgrounds, camp at, 59

Westfall, Harry, 69

When Love Is Dead (Hirabayashi), text of, 155–56

White River Garden, 16, 17, 20, **23**, 30

"Why I Refuse to Register for Evacuation" (Hirabayashi), xiv, 63–64, 66

Wilkening, Joe, 143

Winston, Alex, 96

Wirin, A. L., 147

Wisdom of the Chinese, 156

Wogman, Lela, 143

Wong, Benson, 183

Woodbury, M. D., 45, 46, 47, 71

Woolman, John, 105, 106

WRA. *See* War Relocation Authority
writ of error *coram nobis,* xi, xiv, xv,
    177, 181, 187; pursuing, 167, 176,
    182, 183, 185

Yamada, George, 107, 108
Yanagimachi, Makoto, 140
Yasuharu, Miyabara, 30
Yasui, Min (Minoru), xiv, 62, 123, 130,
    182
Yasui v. U.S. (1943), 182
"Yellow Peril" stereotypes, 126
YMCA International World Brother-
    hood Program, 46–47
Young Men's Christian Association
    (YMCA), 31, 47, 50, 51, 55, 57, 58, 59,
    60, 64, 67, 71, 77, 139; defense com-
    mittee and, 69–70; at UW, 44–45
Young People's Christian Conference
    (YPCC), 31; photo from, **36**
Young Women's Christian Association
    (YWCA), 47, 71

THE SCOTT AND LAURIE OKI SERIES IN ASIAN AMERICAN STUDIES

From a Three-Cornered World: New and Selected Poems
    by James Masao Mitsui

Imprisoned Apart: The World War II Correspondence of an Issei Couple
    by Louis Fiset

Storied Lives: Japanese American Students and World War II
    by Gary Okihiro

Phoenix Eyes and Other Stories by Russell Charles Leong

Paper Bullets: A Fictional Autobiography by Kip Fulbeck

Born in Seattle: The Campaign for Japanese American Redress
    by Robert Sadamu Shimabukuro

*Confinement and Ethnicity: An Overview of World War II Japanese American
    Relocation Sites* by Jeffery F. Burton, Mary M. Farrell, Florence B. Lord,
    and Richard W. Lord

Judgment without Trial: Japanese American Imprisonment during World War II
    by Tetsuden Kashima

Shopping at Giant Foods: Chinese American Supermarkets in Northern California
    by Alfred Yee

*Altered Lives, Enduring Community: Japanese Americans Remember Their
    World War II Incarceration* by Stephen S. Fugita and Marilyn Fernandez

Eat Everything Before You Die: A Chinaman in the Counterculture
    by Jeffery Paul Chan

Form and Transformation in Asian American Literature
    edited by Zhou Xiaojing and Samina Najmi

Language of the Geckos and Other Stories by Gary Pak

Nisei Memories: My Parents Talk about the War Years
  by Paul Howard Takemoto

Growing Up Brown: Memoirs of a Bridge Generation Filipino American
  by Peter Jamero

*Letters from the 442nd: The World War II Correspondence of a Japanese
  American Medic* by Minoru Masuda; edited by Hana Masuda
  and Dianne Bridgman

Shadows of a Fleeting World: Pictorial Photography and the Seattle Camera Club
  by David F. Martin and Nicolette Bromberg

Signs of Home: The Paintings and Wartime Diary of Kamekichi Tokita
  by Barbara Johns and Kamekichi Tokita

Nisei Soldiers Break Their Silence: Coming Home to Hood River
  by Linda Tamura

A Principled Stand: The Story of Hirabayashi v. United States
  by Gordon K. Hirabayashi, with James A. Hirabayashi
  and Lane Ryo Hirabayashi